T0195915

ANGELS:
HERALDS OF GOD

ROBERT F. FELLER

WESTBOW
PRESS®
A DIVISION OF THOMAS NELSON
& ZONDERVAN

Copyright © 2024 Robert F. Feller.

All rights reserved. No part of this book may be used or reproduced by any means, graphic, electronic, or mechanical, including photocopying, recording, taping or by any information storage retrieval system without the written permission of the author except in the case of brief quotations embodied in critical articles and reviews.

WestBow Press books may be ordered through booksellers or by contacting:

WestBow Press
A Division of Thomas Nelson & Zondervan
1663 Liberty Drive
Bloomington, IN 47403
www.westbowpress.com
844-714-3454

Because of the dynamic nature of the Internet, any web addresses or links contained in this book may have changed since publication and may no longer be valid. The views expressed in this work are solely those of the author and do not necessarily reflect the views of the publisher, and the publisher hereby disclaims any responsibility for them.

All Scripture quotations are taken from The Holy Bible, New International Version®, NIV® Copyright © 1973, 1978, 1984, 2011 by Biblica, Inc.® Used by permission. All rights reserved worldwide.

Any people depicted in stock imagery provided by Getty Images are models, and such images are being used for illustrative purposes only. Certain stock imagery © Getty Images.

ISBN: 979-8-3850-1623-5 (sc)
ISBN: 979-8-3850-1738-6 (hc)
ISBN: 979-8-3850-1624-2 (e)

Library of Congress Control Number: 2024901217

Print information available on the last page.

WestBow Press rev. date: 01/23/2024

In Memoriam

To my dear wife of sixty years, Elaine, who inspired the writing of my second book.

Elaine's soul was summoned from this veil of tears to Jesus in heaven on May 22, 2023.

She would say, with the apostle Paul, "For me to live is Christ, and to die is gain" (Philippians 1:21).

CONTENTS

INTRODUCTION

I have been in the ministry for sixty-four years as a Lutheran pastor and have studied dogmatics and doctrine many times. I have a curiosity and a drive to pursue an intensive but comprehensive study of angels.

If we were to take a mike to the streets of either Chicago or New York and ask the people what their concepts are of an angel, I imagine there would be myriad answers—some possibly would be correct, but others might shrug their shoulders and say, "What are you talking about, man?"

I belong to a small but growing mission congregation that another retired pastor and I started five years ago, and we now also have a young, caring pastor. On December 5, 2021, I administered this "Angel Quotient" quiz to the congregation, which included teenagers, young adults, middle-aged and senior citizens, and three Lutheran pastors. Most of the true-or-false questions were quite easy, but others were not. Here are the results:

Members had some difficulty with the illocal presence of angels; angels assuming human form; the day of creation when angels were created; guardian angels; and especially the number of times angels are recorded in the Bible—no one had the correct answer to that question. When asked to list examples of angels in the Old Testament and the New Testament, they drew a blank. I mentioned that I was not looking for one answer, as the Bible has a plethora of examples to choose from the scriptures.

Let us discuss the opinion poll. As children, their concepts of angels included a human form or white being with wings and halos; smiling, chubby cherubs with harps; invisible beings; and God's helpers, who were guardians.

As adults, the members' concepts of angels were of strong messengers of God and soldiers; that they are all about us; and that they are spirits or spiritual beings that protect us from evil.

How did they score on their general knowledge of angels? It was 50 percent little knowledge and 50 percent sketchy knowledge. Several people had no answer. Let's see how you do with the Angel Quotient quiz that follows.

I have inserted humor throughout my book for the entertainment and enjoyment of my readers.

ANGEL QUOTIENT QUIZ

Answer true or false:

1.	Angels have an illocal presence.	T F
2.	At creation, all angels were created holy.	T F
3.	Angels have five wings and polish their halos daily at the "Dr. Pepper hours" of ten, two and four.	T F
4.	At times, God allows His angels to temporarily assume human form to serve Christians.	T F
5.	Angels were created on the second day.	T F
6.	Angels are sexless, for they do not multiply.	T F
7.	At creation, there was a set number of angels and still is, even now.	T F
8.	As Christians, we all have guardian angels.	T F
9.	Angels are mentioned 300 times in the Bible.	T F
10.	Michael, Gabriel, and Raphael are angels in the Bible.	T F
11.	Angels are great basketball players, for they fly up and do slam dunks.	T F
12.	Because angels are holy, they have knowledge of the future.	T F

Write down two examples of angels in the Old Testament

    1.

    2.

Write down two examples of angels in the New Testament.

    1.

    2.

(Answers on page 131 and 132)

ANGEL OPINION POLL

1. Describe your childhood concept of an angel.

2. Describe your concept of an angel now.

3. Presently, how much do you know about angels?
(Choose one)
Nil ____
Bits and pieces ____
A little ____
A lot ____

I have an insatiable desire to read this book and learn more about angelology and the role angels have in my life. Yes ____ No ____

CHAPTER ONE

HERALDS AND ANGELOLOGY

What is a herald?[1] It is a person who proclaims or announces significant news. Other terms used are *harbinger, messenger,* and *forerunner.* In this book, we will study intensively angels as *angelos* (messengers). What role do angels have in the lives of Christians? Angels are proclaimers.[2] To *proclaim* is to declare or to publish abroad.[3] The word *herald* appears in Hebrew, such as herald,[4] ambassador,[5] and messenger. Christian hymnody is replete with references to angels.[6] According to some scholars, angels are recorded in three hundred Bible locations.

Christians ask, "When were angels 'created'?" We do not know the day. We can only postulate that angels were created sometime within the *hexaemeron* (six days of the creation).

Christians also ask about personal guardian angels, "Is a certain angel assigned by God to every believer for his or her protection?" Not

---

[1] Greek is kerux
[2] Greek, kataggeleus
[3] Greek, diaggello
[4] Hebrew, karoz
[5] Hebrew, tsiyr
[6] Hebrew, malakhim

1

just one but many good angels are given to the individual believers for their protection; this is clearly stated in scripture. Whether a certain angel, however, is assigned to every single believer from the day of his or her birth as that person's guardian––as well as whether the guidance and government of the church is assigned to certain angels and whether a special angel presides over providence––is partly uncertain and partly false.[7]

Therefore, we conclude that Christians do not have a personal guardian angel.

In the early 2020s, *Redbook. Ladies' Home Journal,* and *Time* magazines published articles about angels. In 1994, ABC featured a two-hour program called *Angels: The Mysterious Messengers.* On November 28, 1994, an article was published, titled "In Search of the Sacred." We must be cognizant of the fact that angels are ministering spirits, sent out by God to those who will inherit salvation.

The term *host*[8] is ascribed to these heavenly messengers. This term presents four concepts:

1. God's angels engage in spiritual warfare (Psalm 89:6, 8; 1 Samuel 1:11, 17:45).
2. A multitude of heavenly beings surrounds and serves God (Isaiah 6:3f; Revelation 12:7).
3. Angels are messengers of God (Daniel 9:22; Luke 1:11, 26; 2:9; Revelation 1:1).
4. Angels are ministers to God's people (Hebrews 1:14).

A Modern-Day Disaster

In December 2021, a devastating tornado practically leveled a small town in Kentucky. Many lives were lost, but some were saved. Several survivors related that they huddled in an inner steel

---

[7] Quenstedt I, 686
[8] Tsaba, Hebrew, armies, hosts. A military term to denote warfare.

compartment, while others took refuge in a bathtub. President Biden and First Lady Dr. Jill Biden visited the decimated area. He promised all aid would be given for the town to rebuild their homes.

I was a native of St. Louis until I was twenty-six and received my first divine call to serve congregations in South Dakota. When I was a young person, living on West Florissant Avenue, I saw a huge black tornado cloud coming from the Bellefontaine Cemetery across the street. It didn't hit our area but destroyed the arena on Oakland Avenue, numerous miles away. Where were the angels?

Sometimes, we try to second-guess God's divine will. God may protect, provide, and encourage us through His angels, but it does not always guarantee a deliverance. We must keep in mind that God does not always deliver us from danger or come to our rescue in miraculous methods, whether by angels or by His direct intervention. According to His wise will, the opposite may occur (Hebrews 11:36–40).

The Personalities of Angels

What are the personalities of angels?

- Intellect (1 Peter 1:12)
- Emotions (Luke 2:13)
- Will (Jude)––able to leave their first estate

The Nature of Angels

- Angels are spirit beings (Hebrews 1:14) who are capable of taking on physical form (Revelation 18–19).

  We have the account of angels visiting Abram in Genesis 18:1–5.

  In his book *Angels: God's Secret Agents,* Billy Graham writes,

Dr. S.W. Mitchell, a celebrated Philadelphia neurologist, had gone to bed after an exceptionally tiring day. Suddenly he was awakened by someone knocking on his door. Opening it he found a little girl, poorly dressed and deeply upset. She told him her mother was very sick and asked him if he would please come with her. It was a bitterly cold, snowy night, but though he was bone tired, Dr. Mitchell dressed and followed the girl. As Reader's Digest reports the story, he found the woman desperately ill with pneumonia. After arranging for medical care, he complimented the sick woman on the intelligence and persistence of her little daughter. The woman looked at him strangely and then said, "My daughter died a month ago." She added, her shoes and coat are in the clothes closet there.

Dr. Mitchell, amazed and perplexed, went to the closet and opened the door. There hung the very coat worn by the little girl who had brought him to tend to her mother. It was warm and dry and could not possibly have been out in the wintry night.

Could the doctor have been called in the hour of desperate need by an angel who appeared as this woman's young daughter? Was this the work of God's angels on behalf of the sick woman?[9]

- Angels do not reproduce (Mark 12:25).
- They always appear in masculine form, except in Zechariah 5:9.
- They do not die (Luke 20:36).

---

[9] Graham, Billy, Angels: God's secret Agents, Doubleday & Company, Inc. Garden City New York, 1975, page 3.

- They are distinct from human beings (Psalm 8:4–5).
- They have great power (2 Peter 2:11).

Angels' Assurance to Believers

- Angels help believers in general (Hebrews 1:14).
- They are involved in answering prayers (Acts 12:7).
- They give encouragement (Acts 27:23–24).
- They are guardian angels (Hebrews 1:14; Matthew 18:10).
- They observe Christians' experiences (1 Corinthians 4:9; 1 Timothy 5:21).
- They are interested in evangelistic efforts (Luke 15:10: Acts 8:26).
- They care for believers at death (Luke 16:22; Jude 9).
- They are not to be worshipped or prayed to (Colossians 2:18;[10] Revelation 22:8–9).
- They may have contact with humans without their knowledge (Hebrews 13:2).

We believers will judge angels (1 Corinthians 6:3). Either we will condemn evil angels, or we will rule over holy angels.[11]

Disaster to Unbelievers

Michael is Israel's guardian (Daniel 12:1). Angels punish unbelievers (Acts 12:23). Angels will assist God in the harvest (Matthew 13:39).[12]

Angels have an illocal presence; they can only be in one place at one time. God is omnipresent.

---

[10] Angelology, the doctrine of angels.
[11] Ibid
[12] Ibid

5

The Vigilance of Angels

The scriptures exemplify that angels are vigilant, especially in regard to observing God's plan of redemption for humankind. What are the objects of the angel's vigilance?

- They observe God's creation and rejoice (Psalm 38:7).
- They rejoice at the birth of Christ (Luke 2:13–14).
- They see the entirety of Jesus's life on the earth (1 Timothy 3:16).
- They rejoice when a sinner repents (Luke 15:10).
- They observed God's redemptive plan (1 Peter 1:12; Eph. 3:10).

Paul, in Ephesians 3:10, references "things into which the angels long to look." This refers to our salvation. The Greek *parakupto* means "to bend over." This is what John, Peter, and Mary did at the empty tomb on Easter morn.[13]

PhD

It takes eight years of matriculation to obtain a PhD. Just think of the difficult classes that candidates are required to take. Statistics is a most difficult subject. One time, Leon, a PhD, was invited to attend a Christmas party at the local university in his city. The other PhDs introduced themselves and revealed their fields of endeavor.

"Tell us, Leon," one said, "what do you have your PhD in?"

Leon paused for a moment and replied, "Let's have dinner, and when we are sipping our brandy and smoking our cigars, then I will reveal the field of my PhD."

The other professors became very anxious. Leon, smoking his cigar, said, "I am a PhD––a professional hairdresser."

---

[13] Angelology: The Doctrine of Angels, Bible.org

The other professors were shocked, to say the least. From this story, we can learn not to assume anything.

But angels, God's divine messengers, have perfect credentials and serve God night and day in heaven. Hold on to your "PhDs" (pleasant heavenly dwellings).

Go and Tell

During my junior college days at St. John's College in Winfield, Kansas, I joined an evangelistic group called Go and Tell. Our classes were from Tuesday to Saturday morning. Therefore, we had the weekend to visit Lutheran churches around Kansas and present mission skits. There were ten of us men and women, and we assumed different roles each time. At the end of every skit, we gave our personal testimony of our faith.

My personal testimony was Romans 8:38–39:

> "For I am convinced that neither death nor life, neither angels nor demons, neither the present nor the future, nor any powers, neither height nor depth, nor anything else in all creation, will be able to separate us from the love of God that is in Christ Jesus our Lord."

How many angels are recorded in the scriptures? Daniel 7:10 says, "Thousand thousands ministered to Him, and ten thousand times ten thousand stood before Him." Angels are certainly numerous, but the Bible speaks about certain angels and their functions. Let us study these specific angels.

Michael, the Archangel

The name Michael, from the Hebrew, means "who is like God." He is an archangel, meaning he is the chief of all angels and plays a great role in serving God. Some scholars believe that at the creation of angels, Lucifer was an archangel, until he became jealous of God's power and was thrown into hell. What role did Michael play in Old Testament history? In Daniel 10:21, he is called "Michael, your prince," while Daniel 12:1 has reference to "Michael as the Great Prince."

Who will blow his horn on Judgment Day? It certainly will not be Louis Armstrong or Gabriel, but Michael will give a strong cry at the parousia of Christ.

Revelation 12:7–9 cites a war in heaven, where Michael defeats Satan and where Lucifer is cast out of heaven with the fallen angels.

At the University of Bonn in Germany, there is a statue of the archangel Michael staying Satan as a dragon. Inscribed on his shield is "Quis ut Deus." The Anglican and Methodist Churches contend that there are four archangels: Michael, Raphael, Gabriel, and Uriel. The scriptures only record the one and only Michael.

Michael, the archangel, is mentioned in Jude 9. But even the archangel Michael, when he was disputing with the devil about the body of Moses, did not dare to bring a slanderous accusation against him but said, "The Lord rebuke you!"

Gabriel

Gabriel's name, from the Hebrew, means "hero of God." He is often referred to as the messenger of God and is mentioned four times in the Bible (Daniel 8:16; 9:21; Luke 1:19, 26). Gabriel is always associated with being the announcer of good news.

> While I, Daniel, was watching the vision and trying to understand it, there before me stood one who looked like a man. And I heard a man's voice from the Ulai calling, "Gabriel, tell this man the meaning of the vision." And he came near the place where I was standing, I was terrified and fell prostrate. "Son of man," he said to me, "understand that the vision

concerns the time of the end." While he was speaking to me, I was in a deep sleep, with my face to the ground. Then he touched me and raised me to my feet.

He said: "I am going to tell you what will happen later in the time of wrath, because the vision concerns the appointed time of the end. The two-horned ram that you saw represents the kings of Media and Persia. The shaggy goat is the king of Greece, and the large horn between this eyes is the first king. The four horns that replaced the one that was broken off represents four kingdoms that will emerge from his nation but will not have the same power.

"In the latter part of their reign, when rebels have become completely wicked, a stern-faced king, a master of intrigue, will rise. He will become very strong, but not by his own power. He will cause devastation and will succeed in whatever he does. He will destroy the mighty men and the holy people. He will cause deceit to prosper, and he will consider himself superior. When they feel secure, he will destroy many and take his stand against the Prince of princes. Yet he will be destroyed, but not by human power." (Daniel 8:15–25)

Ezekiel and Daniel are the most difficult books of the Old Testament due to the numerous visions. In Daniel 9:15, the term *gaber* (in Hebrew) means "man having the appearance of a man." *Gaber* is given to the angel Gabriel. Daniel 8:15–25 is the first time that an angel is given a name. In Daniel 10, Michael is named. Gabriel definitely is the harbinger of God to bring messages to God's people. He is a lot faster than a package mailed at the post office.

Daniel speaks of the "Prince of princes," which has reference to Christ in His Second Coming on Judgment Day.

Daniel, through this vision, foretells the downfall of Belshazzar's empire. We can learn from Daniel that God's messengers are the holy angels of God who do not seek their own glory but always have God's honor and glory at the forefront. What about us? As sinful human beings, we do just the opposite—we want the power, honor, and glory.

Let us change our ways!

The Second Appearance of Gabriel

Gabriel appears the second time in Daniel 9:21–27:

> While I was still in prayer, Gabriel, the man I had seen in the earlier vision, came to me in swift flight about the time of the evening sacrifice. He instructed me and said to me, "Daniel, I have now come to give you insight and understanding. As soon as you began to pray, an answer was given, which I have come to tell you, for you are highly esteemed, Therefore, consider the message and understand the vision: Seventy sevens are decreed for your people and your holy city to finish transgression, to put an end to sin, to atone for wickedness, to bring everlasting righteousness to seal up vision and prophecy and to anoint the most holy.
>
> "Know and understand this: From the issuing of the decree to restore and rebuild Jerusalem until the Anointed One, the ruler, comes, there will be 'seven 'sevens' and sixty-two 'sevens'. It will be rebuilt with streets and a trench, but in times of trouble. After the sixty-two 'sevens', the Anointed One will be cut off and will have nothing. The people of the ruler who will come will destroy the city and sanctuary. The end will come like a flood: War will continue until the end, and desolations have been decreed. He will

confirm a covenant with many for one 'seven', but in the middle of that 'seven' he will put an end to sacrifice and offering. And one who causes desolation will place abominations on a wing of the temple until the end that is decreed is poured out on him."

Gabriel predicts judgment upon Israel, but there is the great message of restoration. The Anointed One, who is Christ, will come to judge the world with all of His holy angels on Judgment Day. In this vision that is sent through God's ambassador, the prophecy reveals the destruction of Jerusalem. Seven and seventy are biblical numbers to denote perfection or completeness. After the destruction of Jerusalem, Nehemiah and other prophets will start to rebuild. Daniel doesn't state Nehemiah, but in studying biblical history, we know there were great struggles to rebuild Jerusalem. By the synergy of the workers and the zeal of Nehemiah, the walls of the city were completed. It was difficult to rebuild due to enemy forces that attempted to stop the restoration. It took fifty years for the restoration. In 586 BC, Nebuchadnezzar destroyed Jerusalem, and this started the predicted Babylonian captivity. The second temple was destroyed by Titus in AD 70.

Gabriel's Third Appearance

The third appearance of the angel Gabriel is recorded in Luke:

The angel answered, "I am Gabriel. I stand in the presence of God, and I have been sent to speak to you and tell you the good news. And now you will be silent and not able to speak until the day this happens, because you did not believe my words, which will come true at their proper time." (Luke 1:19–20)

Here, the angel Gabriel is telling Zechariah that his wife, Elizabeth, will give birth to a son, who will be John the Baptist.

When John the Baptist was born and Zechariah spoke his name of John, then the priest could speak again. In Luke 1:67–79, Zechariah reveals a great prophecy of the role of John the Baptist. He would be the harbinger who prepared the way for Christ.

As we study the holy scriptures, we see that an angel appears to not only alert his subject but to assure us that God has a plan of salvation for all.

Fourth Appearance of Gabriel

The fourth appearance of Gabriel is noted in Luke 1:26–28, where Gabriel announces the birth of Jesus:

> In the sixth month, God sent the angel Gabriel to Nazareth, a town in Galilee, to a virgin pledged to be married to a man named Joseph, a descendant of David. The virgin's name was Mary "Greetings, you are highly favored! The Lord is with you."

Gabriel assured her that she shouldn't be afraid and should firmly believe Gabriel that this birth would take place. Mary visited her cousin Elizabeth, the mother of John the Baptist. Mary sang her beautiful canticle, called the Magnificat (Luke 1:46–55).

Seraphim

Isaiah 6 mentions *seraphim*; the term means "burning ones." Seraphim are the highest class of angels who sing praises continually to God in heaven. They are always worshipping God. They have six wings and human hands and voices (Isaiah 6:2–7). Why did the seraphim have so many wings? Wouldn't one powerful set of wings be more efficacious? Let us review their six wings—the method by which the Lord created them. Four wings were used for praising God and the remaining two were for service to God.

Some believe that all angels have wings to fly and to move quickly. Not so. Only two wings of the seraphim were used for flying. Sometimes artists portray seraphim in red due to their nomenclature of "burning ones."

Cherubim

Some people today, even Christians, associate cherubim with the small cuties with bows and arrows, as displayed in Valentine's Day cards. How did people get this false concept of cherubim? It probably started years ago in Christmas Sunday school pageants, when little children were dressed up to portray cherubs—they certainly were "cuties." The first biblical account of cherubim is in Genesis 3:24, where God stationed cherubim at the entrance of the garden of Eden, brandishing flaming swords at the expulsion of Adam and Eve from Eden. The word *cherub* denotes "to guard." The cherubim appear atop the ark of the covenant, which denotes that they are guarding (Exodus 25:18–22).

In Ezekiel 1:1–18, the prophet describes these living beings as *cherubim,* depicted as having four faces—one of a man, one of an ox, one of a lion, and one of an eagle. The four designations remind us of the four Gospel writers. They have four conjoined wings that are covered with eyes. Cherubim are recorded in Genesis, Exodus, 2 Chronicles, Ezekiel, and 1 Kings. Cherubim are often termed "throne angels," for they are around the throne of God to guard God's domain. Second Chronicles 3:10–14 describes the two cherubs in the holy place and that their wing span is fifteen feet.

We note that the cherubim gave permission to the high priest to enter the Holy of Holies to plead for God's people. First Timothy 2:5 reads, "For there is one God and one mediator between God and men, the man Christ Jesus."

Notice the clear message that the angelic host proclaimed on the first Christmas Eve. *Peace.* Why isn't peace in the world today? Why are nations warring against one another? Is there any solution?

The United Nations was established years ago to try to ensure peace throughout the world. This is a most difficult—an almost impossible—job!

My wife and I visited the United Nations building in New York City on our honeymoon some sixty years ago. We were impressed with the dedication of the delegates.

CHAPTER TWO

HERALD OF JOY

Would you like to hear good new s throughout your entire life? Of course you would. But in this life of sin, with all of its temptations, good news is difficult to find.

Not so in the scriptures.

> But the angel said to them. "Do not be afraid. I bring you good news of great joy that will be for all people. Today in the town of David a Savior has been born to you: he is Christ the Lord." (Luke 2:10–11)

When angels appeared to a person, they always greeted that person with either "Fear not" or "Don't be afraid."

Why be fearful? The angel is God's messenger. We become fearful because we are unholy sinners, and they are holy. FEAR can be an acronym for false expectations appear real.

To whom did the angel make this great announcement? Did he speak to kings and wealthy people of that day? Not at all. The angel made this wonderful proclamation to the lowly shepherds that night. They were the very lowest of society and the poorest. Even today, although God speaks to everyone, the Lord has a special love and concern for the down-and-out.

Do you feel lonely or fearful, as if God has forgotten you?

So do not fear, for I am with you, do not be dismayed, for I am your God. I will strengthen you and help you, I will uphold you with my righteous hand. (Isaiah 41:10–11)

In these situations, we turn to the Lord in faith. The acronym FAITH stands for fruitful acts independently touch humans.

Happiness

Ted Lewis, a nightclub singer of past decades, would come on the stage in his tuxedo, top hat, and cane and ask the audience "Is everybody happy?" The audience would respond, "Yeah! Yeah! Yeah!" Honestly, were all of the people happy? That's very doubtful.

Job is a classic example of loss and suffering. The devil confronted God and said, in essence, "Your servant Job is too confident and wealthy. What will he be like when he has to suffer the loss of flocks or children or has physical pain?" God said, "But you must spare his life."

Job lost everything. His three friends came to him with some great logic but poor Christianity. Job's first so-called friend, Bildad, makes an appeal to tradition. Find out what their fathers learned about the penalty of their sin. Job gave his reply. Job 9 speaks of the omnipotence, wisdom, and sovereignty of God. Zophar contends he knows exactly what God thinks; he appeals to his own view of God. Eliphaz appeals to experience and observation.

Job's friends searched for a logical reason for Job's suffering.[14]

---

[14] Some scholars say Job suffered from leprosy. But according to recent medical research the disease was scabies, characterized by deterioration in the general condition, with extensive pain, confusion, skin eruptions, and bilious vomiting. Appleboom, Cogan, Klastersky, Job of the Bible: Leprosy or Scabies? (Los Angeles, Calif, Mount Sinai School of Medicine).

They essentially said that Job was suffering but that God was just and would not allow a person to suffer without reason. Therefore, Job must have done something bad to deserve this suffering.

Job defended himself against the logic of his friends. He said that he was suffering, but he knew he had done nothing to deserve this suffering. Therefore, God had some explaining to do. Job's wife was no help to him at all; she said to him, "Curse God and die." Job's reply to his three friends and wife was, "Though he slay me, yet will I hope in Him. (Job 13:15).

Job said the following very famous words, which have been used countless times as a text for Easter sermons: "I know that my Redeemer lives, and that in the end he will stand upon the earth. And after my skin has been destroyed, yet in my flesh I will see God" (Job 19:25–26).

Job's saga has a great ending—all of his possessions were restored by twice as much. Job repented and prayed for his friends. We, like Job, must pray for those who cause us to suffer.

What about our lives? We may never have three so-called friends who try to change our thinking by logic, as Job did, but we must be as firm in our faith as Job was. We know that there will be joy through suffering. The material gain that we lose may never be restored, as was Job's, but we know and trust that God does everything according to His time and plan in our lives.

> These are They who have come out of the great tribulation; they have washed their robes and made them white in the blood of the Lamb. (Revelation 7:14)

As parents and grandparents, we want the best in life for our children and grandchildren. But what makes people happy? If a person won the $750 million Powerball, would he or she invest and spend the money wisely? Statistics prove that the average person unwisely spends money.

The question remains: what makes people happy? Is it money, power, prestige, college degrees, large families, faithful spouses? Yes, it could be.

Wherein is true joy? It is in Jesus as our Redeemer.

"Rejoice in the Lord always. I will say it again, Rejoice!" (Philippians 4:4).

REJOICE stands for remember everything Jesus offers individuals comes eternal.

Just think of the thrill and astonishment that the lowly shepherds of Palestine had when the angel brought them the good news––the good news that a Savior was born that night. What would be our response to the angel's message? At times, we would pause and say, "A baby is born every minute. What is the big deal?" That baby was the promised Messiah for whom the world waited for four thousand years.

Are you a patient person? So often we quote the old adage, "O God, give me patience *now*." We think waiting in line around Christmas at the post office for fifteen minutes, waiting for a bus, or waiting for a package to be delivered is a long time. The people of God in the Old Testament waited four thousand years for Jesus, the promised Messiah.

Advent Season

During the season of Advent, Christians prepare for Christmas with the traditional Advent wreath. The wreath consists of a brass or metal circle, depicting that God is eternal; evergreen branches, showing God is our everlasting Lord; red berries for the blood of Christ; and four candles––three purple and one pink. There also is a large white candle in the center. The four colored candles represent the four thousand years the Israelites waited for a Savior. Purple shows royalty; pink denotes joy.

One purple candle is lit each Sunday in Advent. On the third

Sunday, the pink candle is lit to show joy. The large white candle is lit on Christmas Day.

Another traditional Advent item is fun for children—the Advent calendar, which has windows to open, one for each day during Advent.

Difficult Times

We live in a very turbulent world that, at times, seems to disturb everyone. Both the Atlantic Ocean and Pacific Ocean have their stormy seas. Ships have ended up on the rocks, with cargos of gold and silver lost, and many sailors have lost their lives. Many fathoms below, the fish swim in a peaceful and calm area, while above them are the churning waters.

This is the picture of a Christian. All around us are the turbulent seas that seem to engulf us, but below the water—our hearts—there is a peace that passes all understanding. Why do we have such a peace? It is because we are at peace with God through faith in Christ as our personal Savior.

Fiery Persecutions

The first century was a difficult time for Christendom. Nero and Diocletian, ruthless tyrants and both demented, made an attack on the early Christians. Nero arrested Christians and crucified them outside the walls of Rome. As the saying goes, "Nero fiddled while Rome burned." Nero set fire to Rome but blamed the Christians.

Joy in Heaven

God's angels rejoice at the conversion of unbelievers. Do we, as mortals, have the same joy as the angels when a person comes to faith in Jesus Christ and accepts Him as his or her personal Savior? Sometimes, we thank God, but other times, we disregard the occasion. Prison chaplains constantly visit inmates by bringing them the good news and prayers. The inmates repent and believe in Christ as their Savior.

A negative result occurred during the Nuremberg trials, when Nazi war criminals were brought to justice. Rudolf Hess, even after Lutheran chaplains visited him, would not repent; he was hardened and thought he was justified in his contempt and for the atrocities to the Jews. It was a sad state for this war criminal.

Biblical Joy

King David, a great and talented king of Israel, had his sins, indiscretions, and idiosyncrasies, yet in the Jewish synagogues, you will always see the start of David. When I was on a tour of the Holy Land in 2011, our group of Lutheran pastors visited the Old City and found soldiers with machine guns guarding and patrolling the city. We were about two hundred miles from the border of Syria. Today, it is not safe to take a tour of the Holy Land.

David said in Psalm 30:11, "You have turned for me my mourning into dancing; you have loosed my sackcloth and clothed me with gladness."

Luke 15 is termed the "Chapter of the Lost and Found"––the lost coin, the lost sheep, the prodigal son, and the eldest son. The father greeted his prodigal son who returned home, and he said to the eldest son, who was angry, "But we had to celebrate and rejoice because this brother of yours was dead and is alive again; he was lost and is found."

As Christians, even though we may have to suffer diseases, pain, and untimely death, we are convinced, nevertheless, that Christ is present with His true joy for us.

Paul says it very appropriately:

For I consider that the sufferings of this present time
are not worth comparing we the glory that is going
to be revealed to us. (Romans 8:18)

The words of Paul in Philippians 4:4 ring loud and true to a
believer's ear, not only at the Advent season but always: "Rejoice in
the Lord always; again I will say, Rejoice." Do we rejoice at all times?
I'm doubtful. We all have valleys and mountaintops in our lives. The
lows may lead some people to deep depression. Suicides have been
on the rise with our members of the armed forces.

We rejoice as Christians for we know that this terra firma is
not very firm but very shaky. Frank Sinatra, the noted crooner and
recording artist of millions of records, has on his gravestone, THE
BEST IS YET TO COME. Very true! We look past the sufferings to the
joy to be with Christ—*forever* in heaven.

As children of God, we have joy in God's Word, as He has
revealed Himself to us in the holy scripture.

The writer of Psalm 16:11 states, "You make known to me the
path of life; in your presence there is fullness of joy; at your right
hand are pleasures forevermore."

Christ endured the shame and humiliation and the death on the
cross as the Lamb sacrificed for our sins.

But with the precious blood of Christ, a lamb
without blemish or defect. (1 Peter 1:19)

The early Christians endured persecution for the sake of the
gospel. The blood of the martyrs was the seed of the church.
Christianity grew, in spite of the fiery trials. While on the cross,
Jesus could have called upon his angels to spare Him from the
cross, but He didn't. He was looking ahead to the joy of being in
the Father's presence.

Are you experiencing the recent death of a loved one due to
cancer or COVID-19? COVID-19 is on the rise for those who

have not been vaccinated. Joy separates Christianity from the other religions of the world. We have God's Holy Spirit to come to our rescue as the *paraclete*—to rescue us and give us the assurance that Jesus has redeemed us from sin, death, and the power of Satan.

> So with you: Now is your time of grief, but I will see you again and you will rejoice, and no one w ill take away your joy. (John 16:22)

Joy to the World

Isaac Watts, the famous hymn writer, composed "Joy to the World" in 1719; it was based upon Psalm 98. The tune of today is from the 1848 version by Lowell Mason for *The National Psalmist*. The first four notes of the song are the same four notes that begin the chorus of Handel's *Messiah*. (Mason was a great admirer of Handel.) When I was in junior college at St. John's in Winfield, Kansas (a prep school prior to my going to the seminary), I sang in the college choir when we sang the *Messiah* in many of the Lutheran churches in Kansas.

"Joy to the World" is recognized as the most important of the Christmas hymns in the United States. Stanza 2 tells the story:

> Joy to the world! the Savior reigns:
> Let men their songs employ;
> While fields and floods, rocks, hills, and plains
> Repeat the sounding joy,
> Repeat the sounding joy,
> Repeat, repeat the sounding joy.[15]

The Protestant Reformer Martin Luther not only wrote hymns but also sang hymns for his family and the townsfolk. "O Tannenbaum" (German for "Oh, Christmas Tree") is still sung

---

[15] Hymnary.org

around the world today. In Luther's day, the Christmas tree depicted several things. The freshly cut branches meant Christ is a living Lord, while the candles stood for Jesus as the light of the world. Before electricity in the United States, candles were used in homes. A pail of water was at the ready, and men were armed with wet poles to snuff out fires.

The early Christians, who were under persecution, attempted to identify one another by making the sign of the cross in the sand. That was a dead giveaway to Rome, as they recognized it and further persecuted the Christians. "What plan can we devise to confuse the Romans but still identify ourselves as Christians?" They used the sign of a fish, which in Greek is *ichthus*. They used the first letter of ichthus to spell out their secret code to one another. Below is that symbol that saved many lives in the first century.

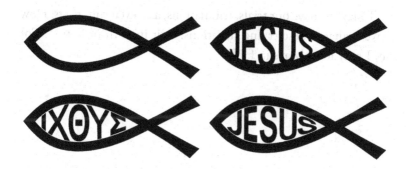

The apostle Peter comforted and strengthened the early Christians during the fiery persecutions under Nero and Diocletian.

> Dear friends, do not be surprised at the painful trial you are suffering, as though something strange were happening to you. But rejoice that you participate in the sufferings of Christ, so that you may be overjoyed when his glory is revealed. (1 Peter 4:12–13)

23

The apostle Paul wrote, "I consider that our present sufferings are not worth comparing with the glory that will be revealed in us" (Romans 8:18).

From Suffering to Joy

Habakkuk, the minor prophet, raised the age-old question that scrutinizes our intellect and faith: "Why do the godly suffer and the ungodly prosper?"

We say life isn't fair, and it is unjust. I agree wholeheartedly from a human point of view but not by a view of faith. God is *never* unfair or unjust. He never forfeits any of His divine attributes at any time. It is our sinful nature that creeps into our lives. We, like Habakkuk, have to sit at the watchtowers of life to determine God's divine answer. For the prophet's day, he received strength and comfort.

Today, we have our trials, tribulations, and even sufferings. How do we manage these trying situations? Is it in faith or fiction? For you, I pray it is always in faith.

CHAPTER THREE

HERALD OF PEACE

On the first Christmas Eve, the angel hosts sang their melodious song of praise, which is recorded in Luke 2:14: "Glory to God in the highest, and on earth peace to men on whom his favor rests."

Throughout the centuries, all Christian churches have sung the hymn "Gloria in Excelsis Deo."

> Glory be to God in the highest, and peace to his people on earth. Lord God, heavenly king, almighty God and Father:
>
> We worship you, we give you thanks, we praise you for your glory.
>
> Lord Jesus Christ, only Son of the Father, Lord God, Lamb of God:
>
> You take away the sin of the world; have mercy on us.
>
> You are seated at the right hand of the Father; receive our prayer,
>
> For you alone are the Holy One, you alone are the Lord, you alone are the Most High, Jesus Christ, with the Holy Spirit, in the glory of God the Father.
>
> Amen.

"Gloria in Excelsis Deo" was often termed the "angelic hymn" due to the opening lines from the anthem sung by the heavenly choir above the fields of Bethlehem when Christ was born. The early church also used the Old Testament, especially from Isaiah 6:3:

> Holy, holy, holy,
> Lord God of Sabbath;
> heaven and earth are full of your glory.[16]

Angels always exalt God and sing joyous anthems of praise to the Lamb. But what about us as human beings? Why can't we always sing, "Glory to God in the highest"? What is wrong with us?

Sinful Mankind

There was a housewife who always maintained a clean and showcase home. The proper colors of paint decorated the walls, furniture was fashionable, and the decor was stunning. But she had a large problem with her kitchen floor. She consulted floor experts in her city to determine the cause. One salesman said, "You are using the wrong floor wax. Try this brand, and it will solve your problem."

That didn't work.

She asked her next-door neighbor, Nellie, for her advice.

Nellie declared, "The problem is simple: you have a dirt floor. Adding more water or other liquid will only make the floor dirtier."

This is the way sin takes a grip on us. We keep on sinning—throwing more water on our dirt floors—which only dirties our lives.

GLORY—God's latest **offering** requiring yield

---

16   Hymnary.org

The Price of Peace

As Christians, we know, accept, and testify to the true meaning of peace. That peace is only through the blood of Jesus Christ, our Savior, who died on the cross to redeem us from sin, death, and the power of Satan. Paul states,

> For God was pleased to have all his fullness dwell in him, and through him to reconcile to himself all things, whether things on earth or things in heaven, by making peace through his blood, shed on the cross. (Colossians 1:19–20)

The apostle Paul reiterates in Romans 15:13: "Now may the God of hope fill you with all joy in believing, so that will abound in hope by the power of the Holy Spirit."

PEACE—-putting eternal attitudes central (easy)

Many pastors use Romans 15:13 as a prayer before the sermon so that the Holy Spirit will fill their souls with joy and peace.

> In peace I will both lie down and sleep,
>   For You alone, O Lord, make me to dwell in
> safety. (Psalm 4:8)

This verse had a special meaning to me as a child, when I attended the funeral of my grandmother Feller in Vandalia, Illinois. Even today, it has great meaning, as I have recited this verse in funerals that I officiated as a Lutheran pastor.

Sans Souci

The term *sans souci* was a popular term in the 1700s in France. It means "without a care" or "without worry." It other words, carefree.

Isn't that the cavalier attitude of so many Americans in our present day––they live without a care?

In one respect, that's good, but in another, it can be wrong. The attitude that is expressed as, "I don't care what happens in this world or to myself." In other words, people become careless in their speech, thinking, and behavior. I want to illustrate by my following diagram:

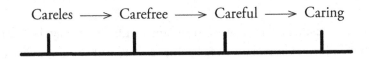

Although a person at times may be careless, there is a good possibility that the person could develop into a caring person.

> *Careless*: Jesus is speaking. "But I tell you that men will have to give an account on the day of judgement for every careless word they have spoken" (Matthew 12:36).

> *Carefree*: On the Sermon on the Mount, Jesus stated, "Therefore I tell you, do not worry about your life, what you will eat or drink; or about your body, what you will wear" (Matthew 6:25a).

> *Careful*: Paul chides the Corinthians, "Be careful, however, that the exercise of your freedom does not become a stumbling block to the weak" (1 Corinthians 8:9).

Caring: Colossians states, "Therefore, as God's chosen people. Holy and dearly loved, clothe yourselves with compassion, kindness, humility, gentleness and patience" (Colossians 3:12).

Too many people surmise that peace denotes a cession of war. Just think of the numerous cease-fire mandates that have been given by numerous countries for a temporary peace. It never works. Why not? The sins of hatred, malice, and lust for power motivate nations to war.

The Alcan Highway

At the beginning of World War II, President Franklin Delano Roosevelt ordered a highway be built to Alaska in order to keep the Japanese troops from our shores. Prior to this highway, there was hardly a road—the signs read, CHOOSE YOUR RUT. YOU WILL BE IN IT FOR 500 MILES.

Due to sin, humankind is always in a spiritual rut, and some do not know how to get out. As Christians, we have the only answer, and that is by claiming Jesus Christ as our personal Lord and Savior.

A Prayer of Peace
May the Prince of Peace give you that peace that passes all understanding. When you have finished your course on earth, may the King of glory welcome you to His glorious kingdom. We pray in Jesus's name. Amen.

Atonement

The temple of Solomon was glorious and resplendent. Today, it would cost a billion dollars to build. It was not only sacrosanct but also very beautiful. No cost was spared. Marble, cedar, gold, silver, and ivory were just some of the materials used in its construction. It was planned accordingly by God. The outer courtyard was the holy place where worshippers could gather. The Holy of Holies was the inner section. Only the high priest on the Day of Atonement could enter and offer sacrifices and intercessions for God's people. He was there for hours and sometimes days. The people asked, "Did the high priest have a heart attack and die?" The high priest emerged, giving his absolution to the people.

A thick curtain separated the Holy of Holies from the holy place. When Christ died on Good Friday, when he offered himself as the supreme sacrifice for the sins of humankind, this curtain was torn asunder, symbolizing that the wall of sin between God and humanity was abolished. Yes, the consequences of sin were paid by the Lamb of God. Now, we are an *at-one-ment* relationship to God by faith in Christ as our Savior.

Prepared?

The Rocky Mountains in Colorado can be a treacherous range of mountains. I found out several years ago when I descended from Estes Park. There were warning signs along the way: USE YOUR BRAKES SPARINGLY WHEN DESCENDING. I found out the hard way when I reached Denver and my front brakes were burned up and had to be replaced.

A more significant sign was PREPARE TO MEET YOUR GOD. I just wonder how many people were prepared to meet their God! Did they have the faith in Jesus Christ as their personal Savior to know that if they died, they would be in heaven? I ask you, my reader––Are you prepared to meet your God?

A Prophetic Message

Isaiah, the great prophet of the Old Testament, foretold of a coming Messiah:

For unto us a child is born, to us a son is given, and the government will be on his shoulders. And he will be called Wonderful Counselor, Mighty God, Everlasting Father, Prince of Peace. Of the increase of his government and peace there will be no end. (Isaiah 9:6–7)

Isaiah foretold the coming of a Messiah thousands of years in advance. The people of the Old Testament longed for a Savior and patiently waited four thousand years for this great event to occur. The prophet twice mentions peace. Christ would bring that peace of the assurance of salvation and heaven through faith in Him as our personal Savior.

Those famous words of Isaiah were used by George Frideric Handel in his greatest oratorio *Messiah,* which is sung by choirs during the Christmas season.

Handel's *Messiah*

Messiah was composed between August 22 and September 14, 1741, and consists of part I, with prophecies from Isaiah, and part II from the Passion, which ends with the Hallelujah chorus. In Part III, Handel depicts the resurrection of the dead and Christ's glorification in heaven. *Messiah* made its debut in 1742 in Dublin. The script was revised and the first published score of Messiah was issued in 1767. The practice of the audience to stand at the Hallelujah chorus was started in 1756 and continues to the present day. Today, such famous choirs as the Mormon Tabernacle Choir and the Royal Choral Society perform the Messiah to large groups.

Shalom

Shalom, in the Hebrew, denotes peace. To the world, peace conjures up an absence of war or other hostilities or freedom from internal strife. The Hebrew root *sim* connotes "to be complete." In the Old Testament as well as today, shalom is a friendly greeting as well as said in goodbyes (Genesis 29:6). It also meant peace from your enemies, and God blessed his people who walked in His ways (Leviticus 26:6). Peace would be a mark of the Messianic era (Isaiah 2:4; 9:6). It depicted an inward peace to the hearts of God's people who trusted the Lord, (Malachi 2:5). Peace elucidates that mode that the godly followed in their lives (Zechariah 8:16, 19).

> *The Aaronic Benediction*
> The Lord bless you and keep you,
> The Lord make His face shine upon you,
> and be gracious to you;
> The Lord turn his face toward
> you and give you peace.
> (Numbers 6:24–26)

Today, in many of the liturgical churches, they substitute the words "face toward you" with "His favor upon you." This is an extremely poor translation of the Hebrew. When I was a student at Concordia Seminary, St. Louis, Missouri, I studied Hebrew for three years. I recently spoke to a Hebrew scholar, and he said "His face to you" is correct. Some churches use the word *countenance*. Let's stay with the Hebrew.

This blessing has been given different names, such as the Birkat Kohanim, the Priestly Blessing, and the Aaronic Benediction. Nota bene: LORD is the sacred tetragrammaton for the Trinity and is used at least 6,500 times in old covenant verses.

And give you peace—yes, this is the item every human being seeks in their lives but seldom finds. Christians have that peace that passes all human understanding, for they know and accept Christ as their personal Lord and Savior.

The Peace Offering

The peace offering is *zebah*. Zebah includes sacrifice of praise, votive offerings, and the free-will offering. A description is given in Leviticus 1:2; 4 and denotes propitiation. Today, people believe that a peace offering is a propitiation for sin. *No!* Christ is the propitiation. Paul states, "God presented him as a sacrifice of atonement, through faith in his blood" (Romans 3:25). The peace offering is called "salvation offering."

Peace, in the Greek *eirene*, has several meanings:

- Harmonious relationship between people (Matthew 10:34).
- Harmonious relationship between countries (Luke 14:32).
- Friendliness (Acts 15:33).
- Freedom from molestation (Luke 19:42).
- Quietness in the churches (1 Corinthians 14:33).
- Relationship between God and humankind. (Ephesians 2:17).

The best version of eirene in the New Testament is a peace that comes to Christians to denote they are at peace with God by sins confessed and forgiven and seeking salvation only through the merits of Jesus Christ.

> Therefore, being justified by faith we have peace with God through our Lord Jesus Christ. (Romans 5:1)

The Pax Romana

The Pax Romana, meaning "peace" in Latin, denotes a two-hundred-year period where Rome expanded its borders, the war years, and competition with Parthia. During this time, the Roman Empire had seventy million people. The Pax Romana began under Augustus in September, 31 BC. He created a junta of military power, and by solidifying them, his forces effectively closed the Gates of Janus (a ceremony showing that Rome was at peace). To the ancients, peace meant when their enemies were defeated and could no longer resist. Augustus, as well as other emperors who followed his lead, had coins produced with the Gates of Janus on one side and Pax on the reverse side.

Peacemakers

Jesus says, "Blessed are the peacemakers for they will be called the children of God" (Matthew 5:9).

As I've mentioned, I took a trip in 2011 to the Holy Land with a group of Lutheran pastors. One of the stops was the Church of the Beatitudes. On the grounds was a beautiful and inspiring chapel that had all of the Beatitudes inscribed above the altar. What are some of practical applications of this passage? Peacemakers desire to reconcile people with God. Peacemakers confront sin in order to develop righteousness.

Years ago, I attended a seminar in order to become a peacemaker. It was an interesting, inspiring seminar. It assisted me in maturing spiritually.

Blessed in the Greek is *makarioi*. Each Beatitude has two sections: the condition and the result. Jesus's words focused on love and humility instead of on force and exaction.

CHAPTER FOUR

HERALD OF SALVATION

At every point of our salvation in scriptures, an angel appears. Why? Let us study this more deeply!

Snapshot One: The Garden of Eden

Adam and Eve were created perfectly without sin, and God allowed them to live forever in His beautiful garden. The garden of Eden was located in Mesopotamia between the Tigris and Euphrates Rivers. Then something tragic occurred—Satan beguiled Eve to eat of the fruit of the tree in the middle of the garden. Eve succumbed and ate and gave fruit to Adam. God sought them out. The Lord made an astonishing prophecy and addressed it to the serpent, who was Satan:

> And I will put enmity between you and the woman,
> and between your offspring and hers; he will crush
> your head, and you will strike his heel. (Genesis 3:15)

This is the first promise of a Savior who would come to save the people from their sins. In this process, the power of Satan would be crushed, but Christ would die on the cross to redeem the world.

Remember that before Adam and Eve sinned, Adam was the most handsome man and Eve the most beautiful woman. But their sin plunged the whole human race into sin, along with flies, mosquitos, cancer, COVID-19, pain, suffering, and death. When doctors graduate from medical school, they have to take a battery of tests to qualify for their state license to practice medicine. One of the intensive tests is on the diseases of humankind.

God banished our first parents forever from the garden of Eden and placed two cherubim with a flaming sword to guard the way to the tree of life (Genesis 3:24).

The world waited four thousand years for the Messiah to come. Oh! What patience the people of old had! What about us? We human beings are so impatient. The promise of the Messiah was proclaimed by the prophets of old to Abraham, Isaac, and Jacob (Genesis 28:15).

Snapshot Two: Jacob

Jacob had traveled many miles in order to flee the anger of his brother Esau. He was exhausted when he arrived at Bethel and fell asleep. He had a dream where he saw a stairway on earth reaching to heaven, and the angels were ascending and descending on it.

The stairway with the ascending and descending angels reminds us that Christ is the only connection to heaven through His precious blood on the cross. Only through Christ's redeeming merits is angelic ministration maintained.

What about our bethels? Do we regard our places of worship as the house of God? The psalmist states,

> One thing I ask of the Lord, this is what I seek: that I may dwell in the house of the Lord all the days of my life, to gaze upon the beauty of the Lord and to seek him in his temple. (Psalm 27:4)

> And he called the name of that place Bethel. (Genesis 28:19a)

Snapshot Three: Announcement to Zechariah

Zechariah was a priest of God, whose wife was Elizabeth. Both w ere very old and had no children. Zechariah was administering his priestly duties in the temple when an angel suddenly appeared, announcing the birth of John the Baptist.

> But the angel said to him: "Do not be afraid, Zechariah; your prayer has been heard. Your wife Elizabeth will bear you a son, and you are to give him the name John." (Luke 1:13)

Gabriel, the angel, said Zechariah would speechless until the birth of John. (How did he communicate daily to the people in the temple? I hope he knew or learned sign language!)

Zechariah; your prayer has been heard. Your wife Elizabeth will bear you a son, and you are to give him the name John." Gabriel, the angel said he would speechless until the birth of John.

How did he communicate daily to the people in the temple? I hope he knew or learned sign language!

HOW IS YOUR MEMORY?

As we get older our capacity to remember items is less and less. Many people take meds to improve their memory while others use extensively smart phones, and buzzers attached to locate lost keys. Older people walk into a room and think to themselves "Why did I come to this room?" A Pastor visited my church and misplaced his smart phone. He almost had a panic attack. It was found. We at times marvel at memory experts that can remember numerous names whom they met only once. It is by attaching a object to the name that will recall the name. Examples: Smith, think of a blacksmith; Jones, Jones' Beach.

SNAPSHOT FOUR: ANNOUNCEMENT TO MARY

The angel Gabriel appeared to Mary and announced that she would give birth to Christ. Mary wondered how could this happen. Gabriel said: "The Holy Spirit will come upon you, and the power of the Most High will overshadow. So the holy one to be born will be called the Son of God." (Luke 1:35).

Mary, at the home of Elizabeth, sang the beautiful canticle of The Magnificat. The first stanza depicts Hebrew poetry or synonymous parallelism when Mary states "my soul" mirrors "my spirit." The second section elecidates the greatness of God and finding delight in God. The third section has three contrasting parallels: the proud are reversed by the low estate, the mighty by those of low degree, and the rich by the emptiness.

MAGNIFICAT- SONG OF MARY

"My soul magnifies the Lord, and my spirit rejoices in God my Savior; For He has regarded the lowliness of His hand-maiden. For behold, from this day all generations will call me blessed. For the Mighty One has done great things to me, and holy is His name; and His mercy is on those who fear Him from generation to generation. He has shown strength with His arm; He has scattered the proud in the imagination of their hearts. He has cast down the mighty from their thrones and has exalted the lowly. He has filled the hungry with good things, and the rich He has sent empty away. He has helped His servant Israel in rembrance of His mercy as He spoke to our fathers, to Abraham and to his seed forever."

The first written variant of the *Magnificat* was in <u>Koine Greek</u>.
[Luke 1:46-55]

SNAPSHOT FIVE: APPEARS TO JOSEPH

Joseph was startled that Mary was pregnant with the Christ Child. He had a thought to divorce her. But an angel appeared to him in a dream instructing him to take Mary home as his wife. The

> their thrones and has exalted the lowly. He has filled
> the hungry with good things, and the rich He has
> sent empty away. He has helped His servant Israel in
> rembrance of His mercy as He spoke to our fathers,
> to Abraham and to his seed forever. (Luke 1:46–55)

The first written variation of the Magnificat was in Koine Greek. (Greek language)

Snapshot Five: Appears to Joseph

Joseph was startled that Mary was pregnant with the Christ child. He had a thought to divorce her, but an angel appeared to him in a dream, instructing him to take Mary home as his wife. The angel said, "Joseph son of David, do not be afraid to take Mary home as your wife, because what is conceived in her is from the Holy Spirit" (Matthew 1:20).

Snapshot Six: The Heavenly Hosts Announce Christ's Birth

Oh! What great news! The Messiah, promised four thousand years ago, has been fulfilled in the birth of Jesus. The angel said, "Today in the town of David a Savior has been born to you; he is Christ the Lord" (Luke 2:11).

Snapshot Seven: Temptation of Christ

This is another snapshot that depicts angels as marking an account of Christ for our salvation. There are two accounts in the scriptures—Matthew's and Luke's. Matthew is more descriptive; he uses Old Testament imagery. Christ was tempted by Satan in the Judaean Desert for forty days and nights.

When I traveled to the Holy Land, our guide pointed out the wilderness, which was barren and desolate. He also showed us the pinnacle of the temple's main tower (Matthew 4:1–11). The numeral forty is significant; it appears several times in the Bible—Israelites wandering in the wilderness for forty years; the flood of forty days; no rain in Israel for forty years; Moses on Mount Sinai to receive the Ten Commandments for forty days; and Egypt's cities will lie desolate for forty years. What were the three temptations of Christ?

1. Make bread out of stones to relieve His own hunger. Jesus replied to the devil, "Man does not live by bread alone, but on every word that proceeds from the mouth of God" (Matthew 4:4).
2. Jump from a pinnacle and rely on angels to break His fall. Jesus rebuffed Satan. "For he will command his angels concerning you to guard you in all your ways; they will lift you up in their hands, so that you will not strike your foot against a stone (Psalm 91:11–12).
3. Worship the tempter in return for all the kingdoms of the world. Jesus responded, "It is also written; Do not put the Lord your God to the test" (Matthew 4:7).

Could you have stood up against these temptations, as Christ did? You might reply, "No! I am not God." True. Remember that Jesus has two natures—the human nature and the divine nature. He was tempted according to His human nature and did not use His divine nature at times.

Satan left Jesus, and angels came and ministered to Him. The terms *ministering* or *served* are often used to show the angels feeding Jesus. Matthew draws the parallel with Elijah being fed by the ravens.

In this story of the temptation of Christ, we see again how the angels are mentioned in the history of our salvation.

Snapshot Eight: The Garden of Gethsemane

All four synoptic Gospels record Jesus's agony in the garden, which was noted for the olive orchard, with all of its oil presses. Gethsemane was located across the Brook Kidron from Jerusalem on the western slope of the Mount of Olives. It was a quiet place and very adaptable for prayer and quietness. Jesus took three disciples—Peter, James, and John, often called "the inner circle" of disciples—with him. They were also on the Mount of Transfiguration with Christ. (When I toured the Holy Land, we viewed the garden of Gethsemane.)

Three times, Jesus prayed to His heavenly Father that the cup of suffering would be removed from His lips. It was the will of His Father that Christ would have to drink the cup down to its bitter dregs. Jesus prays, "Father, if you are willing, take this cup from me; yet not my will, but yours be done" (Luke 22:42). Jesus submits to the will of His heavenly Father.

What about you? Do you submit to the will of God in your life? I pray that you do.

> At that point, an angel from heaven appeared to him and strengthened him. (Luke 22:43)

Here again, the angel appears to mark another chapter in our salvation.

His sweat was, as it were, great drops of blood falling
down upon the ground. (Luke 22:44)

Snapshot Nine: Resurrection of Jesus

Jesus died on the cross of Calvary on the first Good Friday. At
Jesus's death, His body had to be buried according to Jewish law.
Joseph of Arimathea offered a new tomb for the burial. We confess
in the Apostles' Creed, "He descended into hell." Did Jesus descend
to hell to suffer again? *No!* He descended to hell to proclaim Himself
the victor over sin, death, and the power of Satan!

When I toured the Holy Land, I could see Golgotha from the
Garden of the Tomb. We even walked into one of the tombs, which
was very large––large enough for three burials. But remember, *only*
Jesus was buried in a newly hewn tomb. Early Easter morning,
Mary Magdalene and Salome arrived at the tomb in order to anoint
the body of Jesus. They were startled when they were greeted by an
angel, who said,

> Do not be afraid, for I know that you are looking
> for Jesus, who was crucified. He is not here; he has
> risen, just as he said Come and see the place where
> he lay." (Matthew 28:6)

> Regarding his Son, who as to his human nature was
> a descendant of David, who through the Spirit of
> holiness was declared with power to be the Son of
> God by his resurrection from the dead; Jesus Christ
> our Lord. (Romans 1:3–4)

In this story, an angel appears to the women, bringing the good
news that they have a living Lord.

What did the Resurrection of Christ prove? It proved the following:

1. Christ is the Son of God. "He was declared with power to be the Son of God by His resurrection from the dead" (Romans 1:4).
2. He is true. "Destroy this temple, and I will raise it again in three days" (John 2:19).
3. God the Father accepted Christ's sacrifice for the reconciliation of the world. "If, when we are God's enemies, we were reconciled to Him through the death of His Son, how much more, having been reconciled, shall we be saved through His life!" (Romans 5:10).
4. All believers in Christ will rise to eternal life. "I am the resurrection and the life. He who believes in Me will live, even though he dies; and whoever lives and believes in Me will never die" (John 11:25–26).

A Miracle

A pastor was telling the story of Lazarus being raised from the dead to a group of university students. One sceptic asked, "Why did Jesus name Lazarus and not every one?" The pastor replied, "Because all would rise." Jesus centers on the individual.

Snapshot Ten: Ascension of Our Lord

The ascension occurs forty days after Easter according to the liturgical calendar. The death, Resurrection, and ascension of Jesus are the chief doctrines and the foundation of the Christian faith. The scriptures firmly declare that Jesus ascended into heaven in the presence of all of His disciples.

No one has ascended into heaven but he who descended from heaven, the son of man. (John 3:13)

Jesus spoke the following words to Mary Magdalene after His Resurrection: "Do not hold me, for I have not yet returned to my father" (John 20:17). The ascension completed the exaltation in heaven forever. Christians confess in the Apostles' Creed, "He ascended into heaven, and is seated at the right hand of God the Father almighty."

We are the same at times. We are stubborn and always want our own way to solve life's problems. God works through means and history. Be alert to the avenues He sends to rescue you from a given plight.

Footsteps in the Sand

Two men were walking in the sand. They left their double footprints. Suddenly, there was only one set of footprints. The child of God asked the Lord, "Lord, did you forsake me to be on my own?" The Lord would never do so. He carried the man on His shoulders.

The scriptures speak considerably about trusting in the Lord. Jesus says in Matthew 11:28, "Come to me, all you who are weary and burdened, and I will give you rest."

The psalmist says, "Cast your cares on the Lord that he will sustain you; he will never let the righteous fall" (Psalm 55:22).

Invictus

William Ernest Henley had his leg amputated due to tuberculosis. His other leg also required treatment. For twenty months, he was under the care of Dr. H. Joseph Lister, who saved Henley's leg. But Henley was bitter, stoic, and recalcitrant, and he was a non-Christian. While he was in the hospital, during treatment to save his remaining leg, he wrote the poem "Invictus," meaning "unconquered."

Invictus

Out of the night that covers me
Black as the pit from pole to pole,
I thank whatever gods may be
For my unconquerable soul.
In the fell clutch of circumstance,
I have not winced nor cried aloud.
Under the bludgeonings of chance
My head is bloody, but unbowed.
Beyond this place of wrath and tears
Looms but the Horror of the shade,
And yet the menace of the years
Finds, and shall find, me unafraid.
It matters not how strait the gate,
How charged with punishments the scroll,
I am the master of my fate
I am the captain of my souls.[17]

What a poor philosophy of life and lack of Christianity! Yet this is the philosophy of so many people today. I heard one student say about his lifestyle, "I only believe in psychology!" Too many people think––falsely––that they are the masters of their souls. We only have one Lord and Master, and that is Jesus Christ our Lord.

"I am the captain of my soul"––that person's ship is going to sink, for it can never withstand the storms of life. Jesus is our divine pilot. Years ago, a person could buy an addition to their license plate that read "God Is My Copilot." What about you? Is Christ, all in all, your divine pilot through life's dreary ways?

---

[17]   NOTES Worldwise Hymns, 2010/04/20, Erastus-Johnson-Born

Spiritual Indifference

> At that time I will search Jerusalem with lamps
> and punish those who are complacent, who are like
> wine left on its dregs, who think, "The Lord will
> do nothing, either good or bad." (Zephaniah 1:12)

Judah was just as corrupt, indifferent, and rebellious as the other nations around them. False security leads to indifference, as well as indifference to God and His claims, followed by their sins. God will search everywhere. He knows their sins and will punish them.

What about our society today? We see this promulgated through humankind's indifference to the Word of God. Americans, as the people of Judah, reiterate that God is neutral. He is neither good nor bad. God is God, for He never forfeits any of His divine attributes. The Lord is decisive at all times. As human beings, we are so undecided every day of our lives. We can't decide which car to drive, which suit to wear, or which grocery store to visit.

believe in psychology!." Too many people think falsely that they are the master of their soul. We only have one Lord and Master and that is Jesus Christ our Lord. "I am the captain of my soul. That person's ship is going to sink for it can never withstand the storms of life. Jesus is our Divine Pilot. Years ago a person could buy an addition to their license plate that read "God is my Co-Pilot." What about you!. Is Christ all and all your Divine Pilot through life's dreary ways?

SPIRITUAL INDIFFERENCE

(Zephaniah 1:12) says "At that time I will search Jerusalem with lamps and punish those who are complacent, who are like wine left on its dregs, who think, "The Lord will do nothing, either good or bad." Judah was just as corrupt indifferent, and rebelious as the other nations around them. False security leads to indifference as well as indifference to God and His claims followed by their sins. God will search everywhere and knows their sins and will punish them.

What about our society today? We see this promulgated through mankind indifference to the Word of God.

Americans, as the people of Judah, reiterate God is neutral who is neither good or bad. God is God, for He never forfeits any of His divine attributes. The Lord is decisive at all times. As human beings we are so undecided everyday of our lives. We can't decide which car to drive, which suit to wear, or which grocery store to visit.

BEWARE! SALVATION JEOPARDIZED

Two professional chess players were playing in a national chess match where there was a high prize to the winner. But wait - let us look at the other chess player. He is different. It is Satan who proudly says to the other player who is a Christian: "I got you in a box- checkmate its your move now!" Which way will the Christian move? The stakes are high- his very soul. How would you react?

IS THIS A BARGIN?

Department stores have a once-a-month-bargin-basement-Sale. The elevators and the escalators only go down. I worked at a large department store for several years during my seminary years. Unbeknown to everyone, Satan was at work changing all of the prices of the sales price. He reversed the tags. The cheap merchandise doubled in price. People came by the droves only to find that they had been deceived and they complained.

That is what the Devil does in our lives. Satan snookers us in order to push us to defeat. Don't be snookered!

A DANGER AVERTED

A man employed a painter to paint his boat. They agreed on a certain price as payment. When the painter had removed all of the flaky paint he noticed a small hole. He dilently repaired the hole and completed painting the boat. The next day the children of the boat owner went fishing in the lake. The father was panic-stricken for he thought his children would drown due to the small hole in the boat. His children returned safe and sound. The father was thankful as well as amazed. He went to the painter to give him extra money for repairing the hole that averted the sinking of the boat. The painter said "I saw the hole, repaired it, for I am a Christian where Jesus Christ is not only Savior but the Lord of my life." What a witness!

The Three Solas of the Reformation

October 29, 2017 marked the five hundredth anniversary of the Lutheran Reformation. The three solas are (1) sola scriptura, (2) sola gratia, and (3) sola fide.

Sola scriptura means "scripture alone." This sola was formulated from the concept that certain teachings and practices, especially some teachings and practices during the medieval period of Western Christianity, had no scriptural basis. Consider, for instance, the following words of Jakob Andreae. These words were written as part of an attempt to unify "second-generation Lutherans" in the late 1570s:

> We believe, teach, and confess that the only rule and guiding principle according to which all teachings and teachers are to be evaluated and judged are the prophetic and apostolic writings of ancient or contemporary teachers, whatever their names may be, shall not be regarded as equal to Holy Scripture, but all of them together shall be subjected to it.

Sometimes, Bible readers take things out of context, or they are confused by many of the difficult Bible verses. The rule of good exegesis is to interpret the difficult Bible verses in the light of clear verses. A bumper sticker read, "The Bible Says It, I Believe It, That Settles It."

During the Reformation, Martin Luther stated, "A layman armed with the Word of God is stronger than any pope."

Let us study the first sola—"All scripture is God-breathed."

The Bible declares that the Holy Spirit inspired the holy writers to pen God's holy book. Some regard it as so holy that they never open the Bible to study its contents.

Are you a student of the Word, as are the Bereans? They perused what Paul was preaching. The Berean Bible Society distributes Bibles. The American Bible Society offers scriptures. Luther lamented the fact that the Bible in his day was the Latin Vulgate, which the common folks did not know.

> All Scriptures is God-breathed and is useful for teaching, rebuking, correcting and training in righteousness, so that the servant of God may be thoroughly equipped for every good work. (2 Timothy 3:16–17)

Useful in teaching—The Bible gives us all-sufficient instruction in Christian living. This teaching and instruction applies to teaching the pure doctrine, as revealed in the Bible. The Bible is God's inspired Word, not humanity's word.

Rebuking—Better yet, in the Greek, "a proof" for the purpose of refutation of false teachers. Only when we know the truth can we know the falsehoods taught by the world.

Correction—Improvement, amendment; this refers to the morals of people and how the Word can correct the errors.

Training in righteousness—It instructs us in holy living. The

Holy Spirit guides and directs us to do good works, motivated by faith.

Peter says it very aptly: "For prophecy never had its origin in the will of men, but men spoke from God as they were carried along by the Holy Spirit" (2 Peter 1:21). The Lord, in His wisdom, used the talents and gifts of all the writers of both the Old Testament and the New Testament, but the Holy Ghost gave them the inspired Word.

Today, people want to study the Bible in a cafeteria style, which means they want to pick and choose what they believe and do not believe. This is wrong.

The second sola is *sola gratia,* meaning "grace alone." We are saved solely by the divine grace of God by the merits of Jesus Christ. People of the world have devised other ways of salvation, such as saved by good works, being a good person, trying to be justified by their civic righteousness, and trying to keep all of the Ten Commandments. All of these come to naught and *all* are unscriptural.

An Evangelism Approach

Dr. Kennedy of Coral Ridge Presbyterian Church of Fort Lauderdale, Florida, developed a special evangelism method of reaching out to the unchurched. When callers would visit a family, they would introduce two "Kennedy questions": (1) If you die tonight, will you go to heaven? (2) What would be your answer if the Lord asks, "Why should I allow you into heaven?"

A person will answer the first question with, "Of course I will go to heaven." The answer to the second question might be, "Because I am so good" or "Because of my works." All are wrong! This is the time to witness the grace of God to that family.

Falling Short of the Mark

Paul writes, "For it is by grace you have been saved, it is the gift of God-9 not by works, so that no one can boast" (Ephesians 2:8–9).

Martin Luther, in his early life, was vexed by the heart-searching question, "How can I satisfy a wrathful God?" Later, through the Bible, he learned he could not satisfy' God by fasting, solitude, or beating his body; he had to rely on the grace of God.

> For all have sinned and fall short of the glory of
> God. (Romans 3:23)

Many people enjoy archery. It is an exacting sport that requires precision. The archer draws his large bow, pulls back the arrow, and it flies to the target. Expert archers hit the bull's-eye every time. But think of an archer as spiritually attempting to hit the target of heaven! He pulls back his bow, the arrow flies, but it falls short of the target. So it is, spiritually, for every one who tries to hit the target of heaven by being good or by works. Only through the grace of God, through Christ, are we saved.

The third sola of the Reformation is *sola fides,* or faith alone.

In 1514, in the tower room of Luther's home, he read the words of Romans 5:1 "Therefore, since we have been justified through faith, we have peace with God through our Lord Jesus Christ."

Luther was a troubled monk, spiritually. He turned to his professor friends and asked, "What does this mean?"

The reply was, "No, Brother Martin, we will send you off to Rome, and you will forget this verse."

Luther went to Rome, but what he saw at the Vatican turned his stomach. He thought again of Romans 5:1.

> Der alt bose Feind
> mit Ernst er's jetzi meint,
> grob Macht und viel List
> sein grausam Rustung ist,
> auf Erd ist nicht seins gleichen.

The Protestant Reformation

There were other Reformers, such as Zwingli, Hus, and Wycliff, who attempted to reform the Roman Church but failed. Then Martin Luther came on the scene, and history was in Luther's favor. This was the time of the Peasants' War, a peasant uprising in Germany; Gutenberg's invention of the printing press; Ottoman attacks, which decreased conflicts between Protestants and Catholics; princely patronage; and proximity to neighbors. Until this time, Luther was a dedicated and faithful monk of the Roman Church, but times change.

Pope Sixtus (1471–1484) sent his errand boy Tetzel to sell indulgences, designed to arouse fear among the common people, in order to pray loved ones from purgatory. The main purpose of indulgences was to gain more money to build the pope's lavish churches.

These indulgences so angered Luther that he posted his famous Ninety-Five Theses, in which he criticized the indulgences, purgatory, particular judgment, and the authority of the pope. He posted his theses on October 31, 1517, on the Wittenburg Church. This started the Protestant Reformation. Luther was excommunicated by Pope Leo X on January 3, 1521, by the bull Decet Romanum Pontificem. Then Luther swung into action. He was a marked man at this time. He had princely patrons who hid him at the Wartburg Castle disguised as "Knight George." There, Luther translated many of the Latin works into the German of his day. It was not until 1525 that the Reformation gained momentum by Elector Frederick the Wise, a patron of Luther's.

From 1517 to 1521, Luther wrote items on the Virgin Mary, saints, the sacraments, the authority of the pope, celibacy, ecclesiastical law, the law, good works, and monasticism. This was the time when many nuns left the monastic life. Luther found husbands for most of the nuns, except the nun Katharina von Bora, whom he loved and married.

Martin Luther

If you pictured Luther today, what image would come to mind? I am an alumnus (class of 1958) of Concordia Seminary, St. Louis, Missouri. Across from the main entrance of Concordia is a large statue of Martin Luther holding the scriptures. The Word meant so much to him, as it should to us today. There are other statues of Luther in the world:

- A monument is in the marketplace at Wittenburg, Germany, showing Luther pointing to an open Bible.
- Rietschel's Luther Monument at Worms, Germany, shows Luther resting his head on the Bible.
- A monument in Eisenach, Germany, depicts the Reformer clasping the Bible to his heart with his left hand, while a right hand crushes a letter of indulgence.

Paintings also feature Martin Luther. Two paintings by Lucas Cranach depict Luther with the Bible in his hand. Wilhelm von Kaulbach's *Age of Reformation* places Luther in the center of the canvas, holding the open Bible aloft.

The scriptures meant so much to Luther. What about you?

Bible Chained Down

In Luther's day, the Bible was on display for everyone to see. I say *to see,* for it was the Vulgate, the Latin version that only the scholars understood. Also, the pages were seldom turned to another page. Luther brought the Word of God to the people in their language, which was German.

On October 26, 1980, the United States and England celebrated the two hundredth anniversary of the founding of the Sunday school. Robert Raikes, a newspaper editor in Gloucester, England, w ho had devoted numerous years to the cause of prison reform, opened a Sunday school in 1780. His first attempt was a failure, but in 1791, in Philadelphia, Pennsylvania, the First Day of Sabbath School Society was established. But the blessing of Sunday school is traced to Martin Luther, who was instrumental in encouraging Christian education.

Diet of Worms

THE LUTHER ROSE

The Luther rose

Why is Luther's Rose so important? For centuries it has been a symbol of Lutheranism throughout the world. What is the seal's origin? While Dr. Martin Luther was at the Coburg Fortress in 1530, it was designed by John Frederick of Saxony. It started when Spengler sent Luther a drawing of the seal. Immediately Luther was appreciative that the seal was an expression of his theology.

What does Luther's Rose mean?

The black cross depicts the center of the Reformer's theology.

The black cross in a heart reminds everyone that it faith in Christ that saves.

"For one who believes from the heart will be justified." (Ro. 10:10) The heart is in its natural color. It does not corrupt nature, that is, it does not kill but keeps alive.

The Holy Spirit convinces man of his sin and points him to the Gospel of a crucified and risen Christ. The red heart is superimposed upon a white rose to elucidate that faith gives joy, comfort, and peace in a Christian's life. This white rose is a joyous rose, for this faith does not give peace and joy like the world gives (John 14:27). The rose is white, not red, for white is the color of the spirits and the angels (Matthew 28:3; John 20:12). The Mwite rose is set in a sky-blue background to show the beginning of the heavenly future joy. Around the blue field is a golden ring depicting that such blessedness in heaven lasts forever. Jewelry such as rings, pendants, and necklaces, are sold to depict Luther's Rose.

SHANGHAIED

During the 1880's captains of ships had a most difficult job of recruiting sailors for their ships. A sequel would be today in 2021 when employers are begging people to come to work. They offer higher wages and some would pay their employees by the day. Back to Captain Kaput who employed a bartender to slip a "Mickey" into the drinks of young men that the captain wanted to recruit for his ship. When the men were drugged, they were taken to the boat. When they woke up Captain Kaput, adjusting his pegleg, straighing his eye patch, drawing his sword said: "Welcome abroad you landlubbers. You have been shangaied." I will make sailors of you!"

Satan is always busy in the church to shanghaie us by his temptations in order that we sin and at times feel that God no longer loves us. God always loves us!

faith in Christ. Clearly defined, good works are a fruit of faith in the sanctified life of the Christian.

These are the three solas of the Lutheran Reformation. I pray that you cherish and grow in your faith. We need another Reformation today, so let us lift high the cross of Christ in our hearts, lives, churches, and communities.

What are the blessings of the Lutheran Reformation? They are high schools, Sunday school, parochial school, seminaries, colleges, universities, hospitals, family, universal priesthood of believers, catechism, the Bible in all languages, three solas, missions, separation of church and state, high esteem for the clergy, distinction of law and gospel, marriage, dignity of work, assurance of heaven, authority of the local church, and much more.

The Luther Rose

Why is the Luther rose so important? For centuries, it has been a symbol of Lutheranism throughout the world. What is the seal's origin? When Martin Luther was at the Coburg Fortress in 1530, the seal was designed by John Frederick of Saxony. It started when Lazarus Spengler sent Luther a drawing of the seal. Immediately, Luther was appreciative that the seal was an expression of his theology.

What does the Luther rose mean?

The black cross depicts the center of the Reformer's theology. The black cross in a heart reminds everyone that it is faith in Christ that saves.

> For one who believes from the heart will be justified.
> (Romans 10:10)

The heart is in its natural color. It does not corrupt nature; that is, it does not kill but keeps alive.

The Holy Spirit convinces individuals of their sin and points them to the gospel of a crucified and risen Christ. The red heart is superimposed upon a white rose to elucidate that faith gives joy, comfort, and peace in a Christian's life. This white rose is a joyous rose, for this faith Martin Luther graduated from bread and water as a monk to nourishing food from his dear wife, Katharina von Bora. She noticed that he was gaining pounds and becoming round, so she placed him on a special diet of cheese, fruit, and tea. The pounds really came off, such that he almost had the physique of Arnold Schwarzenegger. But wait––she just added some chocolate-covered worms for his dessert. No, a *diet* referred to the imperial assembly of the Holy Roman Empire in Worms, Germany, that was called by Emperor Charles V. The purpose was that the Roman Church wanted Luther to recant all of his writings.

The diet assembled April 16–18, 1521, and Johann Eck, an assistant of the Archbishop of Trier acted as the spokesman for the emperor. On April 17, 1521, the spokesman asked that the titles of Luther's twenty-five writings be read. On April 18, Luther, after much prayer, answered, "They are all mine; they are not all of one sort." Luther divided his writings into three categories: (1) works that were well received by his enemies, (2) books that attacked the abuse and lies of the papacy, and (3) attacks on individuals.

Then Luther delivered his famous speech:

> Unless I am convinced by the testimony of the Scriptures or by clear reason (for I do not trust either in the pope or in councils alone, since it is well known that they have often erred and contradicted themselves), I am bound by the Scriptures I have quoted and my conscience is captive to the Word of God. I cannot and will not recant anything, since

it is neither safe nor right to go against conscience.
May God help me. Amen.[18]

From that day forward, Luther was declared a heretic, to be apprehended and punished. But under the kind patronage of Frederick III, the king faked a highway attack and abducted Luther to the safety of Wartburg Castle.

Luther took a courageous stand for the gospel. Will you take such a courageous stand today for the gospel?

Las Posadas

Las Posadas (Spanish for "The Inns") is celebrated by the Spanish culture in Latin America, Mexico, Guatemala, Honduras, Cuba, Spain, and the United States. This festival is a reenactment of the Christmas story. A child, dressed as an angel, leads a procession down a dark village street, followed by two others dressed as Mary and Joseph and other children dressed in silver and gold robes, carrying lit candles. Prior to the beginning of the procession, homes along the route are designated as inns with innkeepers. The Holy Family stops at each inn, asking for lodging for Mary, who is about to deliver the Christ child. Each time, they are refused. Many of the innkeepers become incensed and reply, "Don't you know there is a census in town, and all inns are occupied?" Nevertheless, the Holy Family continue to seek lodging. At the last inn, the innkeeper says, "Come in, Holy Family, and make your abode here."

Las Posadas takes place between December 16 and 24, with some variations. At most of the sites, Christmas carols are sung, scripture is read, and prayers are said. At the conclusion, the children

---

18   Brecht, Martin, Martin Luther. tr. James L. Schaaf, Phladelphia: Fortress Press, 1985-1997.

break piñatas, which are crafted as stars to symbolize the wise men visiting the newborn Jesus.

On my tour of the Holy Land with other Lutheran pastors in 2011, we saw numerous biblical sites. Among them was the Church of the Nativity in Bethlehem. Although it is still a small town, millions of tourists from all over the world visit this sacred site. The entrance to the church is quite different. You enter on the ground floor by way of an entrance only four feet high. What was the reasoning for the small aperture? This was devised in ancient times to prevent horsemen from vandalizing the church. When I was there, the church was under a huge renovation. We did climb down the stairs to view the star that pinpoints the exact spot where Jesus was born. It was quite an experience.

Under divine inspiration, Micah 5:2 states,

> "But you, Bethlehem, Ephrathah, though you are small among the clans of Judah, out of you will come for me one who will be ruler over Israel, whose origins are from old, from ancient times."

Each tribe was divided into thousands to denote clans. The ruler who would come would be the Messiah, Christ our Lord. Micah notes that God, in His wisdom, chose a small, insignificant hamlet where the Christ child would be born. Our God utilizes the small, insignificant places to fulfill prophecy.

Away in a Manger

Many historians claim that Martin Luther was the author of the famous hymn "Away in a Manger." The opposite is true in modern research. No text in Luther's writings is related to the carol, and no German text has been found earlier than 1934. When nineteenth-century historians mention a carol that Luther wrote for his son

Hans, they are referring to "Vom Himmel hoch, da komm ich her" ("From Heaven Above to Earth I Come").

In 1895, William J. Kilpatrick penned "Away in a Manger" (then called "Luther's Cradle Song") based upon Luke 2:4–7. On Christmas 1883, it was performed by a Sunday school in Nashville, Tennessee. By 1891, the hymn was very popular in the United States with four musical settings. Murray's melody was used without credit due to Carl Mueller.

> Away in a manger, no crib for a bed,
> The little Lord Jesus laid down his sweet head.
> The stars in the bright sky looked down where he lay,
> The little Lord Jesus asleep on the hay.

Hark! The Herald Angels Sing

This is a world-renown hymn that is sung at Christmas in all Christian churches. The hymn is based on Luke 2:14 and was written by Charles Wesley, founder of Methodism, and adapted by George Whitefield. Mendelssohn composed a cantata to note Gutenberg's invention of the printing press. In 1855, Cummings published an adapted version of Mendelssohn's "Festgesang" to form the lyrics of "Hark! The Herald Angels Sing." Originally, Wesley intended the hymn for an Easter song, "Christ the Lord Is Risen Today."

It Came Upon a Midnight Clear

This hymn was written by Rev. Edmund Sears in 1849 and was based on Luke 2:14. Sears's five-stanza poem was published on December 29, 1849 in the *Christian Register* in Boston, Massachusetts. After he assumed the duties of his larger congregation, First Church of Christ, in Lancaster, Pennsylvania, he suffered a mental breakdown with severe depression. Sears wrote this hymn at the request of his good friend Rev. William Lunt. The hymn was sung at the Sears home on Christmas Eve. Arthur Sullivan adapted the lyrics.

Angels from the Realms of Glory

This Christmas hymn was written by James Montgomery in 1816. Montgomery was born in Scotland in 1771 and died in 1854 in Yorkshire, England. His parents died on the mission field in the West Indies. Montgomery followed in his parents' footsteps with a zeal for missions. He protested slavery, boy chimney sweeps, and lotteries. He was imprisoned for a brief time when he published a song that featured the fall of the Bastille and again when he wrote an article that put an army commander in an unfavorable public image.

Difficult Times

Did two men make a successful escape from Alcatraz? No one knows for sure. Our government says the men drowned, and their bodies were carried out to sea. Alcatraz was officially closed as a prison on March 21, 1963. Millions of tourists visit "the Rock" to see what happened years ago.

Death or Pardon?

A group of notorious cutthroats and gangsters looked out of their miserable, filthy cells and saw and heard their fellow prisoners being killed by the firing squad. They each wondered, "When will my time come? Will I be shot? Will I be pardoned?" None knew for sure. Then the day of reckoning arrived. The criminals were marched from their cells to face their fate. This was crunch time; they were in a tight spot. What would be the outcome?

The captain had a complete list of all the prisoners. Some of the prisoners got a glance at the list; there was a note beside each name. Some had an X while others had a black cross.

"Jimmy John, front and center! By the decree of our governor, who is a Christian man and who placed a cross beside your name, you are pardoned. You are a free man."

Just think of the joy of that former prisoner. He was pardoned from all of his sins.

Today, we are pardoned men and women by the black cross of Christ, signifying sins canceled through the blood of Christ.

> "Blessed is he whose transgressions are forgiven, whose sins are covered. Blessed is the man whose sin the Lord does not count against him and in whose spirit is no deceit." (Psalm 32:1–2)

Inheritance

The Greek word *kleronomia* refers to property as an inheritance: (1) property that passes after death; (2) a portion of an estate made the substance of the gift; (3) possessions of the believer ushered by Christ's return.

Are you waiting to receive a great inheritance from a wealthy uncle who will pass away? Probably not. In this lifetime, we do not have rich uncles who will leave us an earthly inheritance. Forget about the wealth. We are spiritually rich.

> Giving thanks to the Father, who has qualified you to share in the heritance of the saints in the kingdom of light. (Colossians 1:12)

Barbara Hutton

Barbara Hutton, child of Frank Winfield Woolworth, was called "Poor Little Rich Girl." At the height of the Great Depression, she was thrown a lavish $60,000 debutante ball on her eighteenth birthday. She was married seven times, and all of the marriages ended in divorce. One of her famous husbands was Cary Grant. Hutton lived a selfish and lavish lifestyle that finally led to her death at the age of sixty-six. With all of her past wealth, she had only $3,500 in her bank account at the time of her death. She was a spoiled woman from the get-go. Her body was interred in the Woolworth family mausoleum at Woodlawn Cemetery, Bronx, New York.

We might conclude that the rich go to hell and the poor go to heaven. No, not on your life! It depends upon the faith we have in Christ—or faith we do *not* have in Christ. In the book of Matthew, Jesus spoke on numerous topics. On one occasion, he confronted a rich young man who would not part with his wealth. Then Jesus said to His disciples,

> I tell you the truth, it is hard for a rich man to enter the kingdom of heaven. Again I tell you, it is easier for a camel to go through the eye of a needle than for a rich man to enter the kingdom of God. (Matthew 19:23–24)

The disciple of our Lord recognized what Jesus was saying in reference to the camel and the needle. The Needle's Gate is one of the gates used as an entrance to the city of Jerusalem. It is so short that a camel has to crawl on its knees to pass through this gate. So it is with the rich—they must become humble.

CHAPTER FIVE

HERALD OF PROTECTION

Shadrach, Meshach, Abednego

King Nebuchadnezzar had made a decree that when everyone heard the sound of the horn, flute, zither, lyre, harp, pipes, and all kinds of music, they were ordered to bow down and worship the image of gold. Whoever did not bow down would be thrown into fire. Some astrologers in the king's court reported that Shadrach, Meshach, and Abednego did not comply with the king's order. Were God's three men rebels? Yes, with a great cause––to speak up and defend their faith in the one true God. They refused the king's order and were thrown into a furnace seven times hotter. It was so hot that the heat killed the king's henchmen. God's people, however, were spared, and Nebuchadnezzar marveled and attested to the fact in Daniel 3:28. Then Nebuchadnezzar said, "Praise be to God of Shadrach, Meshach and Abednego, who has sent his angel and rescued his servants!" The three were promoted in the king's empire.

What a wonderful story of God's protection for God's servants! We may never be thrown into a furnace of fire due to our faith, but we may be tested by God in other areas of our lives, such as sickness, hospitalization, loss of job, or other items. But we should always take heart that our God is always there to protect us with his holy angel.

Daniel in the Lion's Den

Even in Daniel's time, there were rumormongers who tried to ruin a person's reputation. Some of the satraps went against Daniel. The prophet's name, from the Hebrew, means "God is my judge." A correct title. The satraps went to the law of the Medes and Persians that stated that anyone who did not bow down to an idol would be thrown into the lion's den. They reported to the king that Daniel had violated the king's order. Daniel was thrown into the lion's den to be devoured by hungry lions that had not eaten for days.

What were the thoughts of the lion? The lion thought, "Boy, am I hungry. I haven't eaten in two days! There are a lot of steaks on this guy before me. Lead me to this buffet."

What thoughts did Daniel have? "Lord, I am in a tight spot. I pray that you will deliver me. I trust only in you." God delivered Daniel, for an angel came and shut the mouth of the lion.

That night, King Darius couldn't sleep. The next morning, he visited the lion's den and called out, "Daniel, servant of the living God, has your God, whom you serve continually, been able to rescue you from the lions?" (Daniel 11:20).

Daniel answered,

> O king, live forever! My God sent his angel, and he shut the mouths of the lions. They have not hurt me because I was found innocent in his sight or have I ever done any wrong before you, O king. (Daniel 6:21–22)

Darius was so impressed that he praised the God of Daniel. Could we ever make such a witness upon someone through such an event? We may never be placed in such a tight spot as Daniel, but at times, we have to endure frustrations and tribulations.

Directed by an Angel

Las Vegas, meaning "the meadows," grew greatly throughout the years. Houses went up faster than casinos. The strip was ready for the casinos. The MGM casino had a terrible fire many years ago that caused a terrific inferno that completely destroyed the casino. There was one Christian couple who was trapped and couldn't find their way out. All around them were flames. Suddenly, they saw a man dressed in white motioning to them and saying, "Follow me; this is the way out!" They did, and later, they wanted to thank the man. He had disappeared. Yes, it could have been one of God's ministering angels who rescued this couple.

The Apostles Delivered

The apostles healed many people in their day, and these healings attracted the religious party of the Sadducees, who didn't believe in the Resurrection. They were filled with jealousy, so they had the apostles arrested and thrown into jail.

> But during the night an angel of the Lord opened the
> doors of the jail and brought them out. Go, stand in
> the temple courts" he said, "and tell the people the
> full message of this new life." (Acts 5:19–20)

What a witness the apostles made in that community! What kind of an impact are we making on our communities with our outreach of witnessing? I pray it is very positive.

Rescued by an Angel

The Reverend John G. Paton, a missionary in the New Hebrides Islands, tells a thrilling story involving the protective care of angels. Hostile natives surrounded his mission headquarters one night, intent on burning the Patons out and killing them. John Paton and his wife prayed all during the terror-filled night that God would deliver them. When daylight came, they were amazed to see the attackers unaccountably leave. They thanked God for delivering them.

A year later, the chief of the tribe was converted to Jesus Christ, and Reverend Paton, remembering what had happened, asked the chief what had kept him and his men from burning down the house and killing them.

The chief replied in surprise, "Who were all those men you had with you there?"

The missionary answered, "There were no men there; just my wife and I."

The chief argued that they had seen many men standing guard—hundreds of big men in shining garments with drawn swords in their hands. They seemed to circle the mission station so that the natives were afraid to attack.

Only then did Reverend Paton realize that God had sent His angels to protect them. The chief agreed that there was no other explanation. Could it be that God had sent a legion of angels to protect His servants, whose lives w-ere endangered?

Witness Protection Program

The United States Federal Witness Protection Program, also known as Witness Security Program, was established under Title V of the Organized Crime Protection Act of 1970. The law was passed to protect and relocate witnesses. If the trial is only a few days hence, the witness is usually placed in a safe house until the trial. When the witness gives his testimony at the trial, he is given a new identity, housing, living expenses, medical care, and job and employment aid and is protected twenty-four/seven by US marshals. No one in the program has been harmed or killed.

Just think—if the US marshals have that great record, how

much greater is the record of God's angels who guard and protect us continually? Watch! The angels are guarding and watching over you! Don't drive these messengers of God from your life; welcome them when they intervene in your Christian life.

Disappointment

I shop at the ninety-nine–cent store in our community every month to purchase toothpaste, foil, and sundries. Last year, I bought two boxes of Christ-centered Christmas cards. This year, I was very disappointed when they were only selling cards depicting Santa Claus, Frosty the Snowman, and Rudolph the Red-Nosed Reindeer. Christmas is *Christ*-mas—Jesus's birth! We are living in a very secular world of materialism and selfishness. Jesus is the reason for the season.

Elijah's Despair

Elijah was down and almost out, as he was fleeing to Horeb, away from Jezebel, who had threatened his life. "I have had enough, Lord," he said. "Take my life; I am no better than my ancestors" (1 Kings 19:4c). Then the angel appeared.

> All at once an angel touched him and said, "Get up and eat." He looked around, and there by his head was a cake of bread baked over hot coals, and a jar of water. He ate and drank and then lay down again. The angel came back a second time and touched him and said, "Get up and eat, for the journey is too much for you." (1 Kings 19:5–7)

Our text tells us that the food he ate lasted forty days. There are biblical numerals in the scriptures—three, ten, and forty denote completeness. Here again, we see how the angel not only protected him from Jezebel but, more importantly, ministered to his physical needs. Elijah's name, from the Hebrew, means "My God is the Lord." He often was referred to as the Prophet of Fire when he had a showdown with the prophets of Baal.

Sometimes we are frustrated, depressed, down, and almost out, but then God comes with His strengthening message of direction and confidence for our lives.

Peter Imprisoned

Acts 12:1–10 describes Peter's arrest and his being thrown into prison by King Herod. Herod was a cruel, bitter, and ruthless king of that day. Peter was chained between two soldiers, and sentries stood guard at the entrance of the jail.

> Suddenly an angel of the Lord appeared and a light shone in the cell. He struck Peter on the side and woke him up. "Quickly, get up!" he said, and the chains fell off of Peter's wrists. Then the angel said to him, "Put on your clothes and sandals." And Peter did so. "Wrap your cloak around you and follow me," the angel told him. (Acts 12:7–8)

We learn the angel delivered Peter from the prison and protected him. Notice that the angel said "Follow me." The angel pointed him back to the community for Peter to continue his ministry of preaching the gospel.

A Stormy Sea

Paul, en route to Rome to testify before Caesar, encountered a storm, which was a northeaster that not only shook up passengers but also the boat. This hurricane tossed the boat back and forth to the point of its falling apart. Throughout the journey, Paul encouraged everyone. Julius, who belonged to the Imperial Regiment, allowed Paul to minister to the needs of his fellow prisoners––Paul, at this time, was a prisoner of Rome and was destined to die in Rome.

I was in Rome in 2010 and 2012, and on both occasions, I saw the building where Paul was imprisoned. The building was locked. We read some scripture about Paul and had a prayer on the spot.

Back to the stormy situation––it was nerve-racking and frustrating for all aboard. Paul, says to the men,

> But now I urge you to keep up your courage, because not one of you will be lost; only the ship will be destroyed. Last night an angel of God whose I am and whom I serve stood beside me and said, 'Do not be afraid, Paul. You must stand trial before Caesar; and God has graciously given you the lives of all who sail with you.' (Acts 27:22–24)

Paul had a great faith in frustrating times to meet the challenges set before him by God's guidance and prayer. Think for a moment of God's divine intervention. The Lord allowed the crew to be saved for the sake of Paul, who had to go to Rome to witness before Caesar. What a witness Paul gave to these unbelievers! He testified of what the angel had told him the night before––that no one would be lost.

What about our witnessing to unbelievers? Do we have the courage of Paul? We can, if only we will pray that the Holy Spirit would put the words into our mouths.

ACTS prayer:

Adoration––praise God for who He is and what He has done for you.

Confession––admit your sins of thought, word, and deed.

Thanksgiving––thank God for all He has done and will do.

Supplication––make requests for yourself and others.

"Five Finger" prayer:

Thumb—pray for those closest to you: family members, neighbors, friends, or members of your church family.

Index finger—pray for those who guide others: teachers, doctors, pastors, counselors, social workers, and mentors. They need support and wisdom as they point others in the right direction.

Middle finger (tallest one)—pray for those who stand tall: our president; government, civic, and business leaders; police and firefighters.

Ring finger (your weakest finger)—pray for those who are weak: the poor, sick, infants, homeless, and the powerless.

Pinky (the smallest, the least)—pray for yourself and for your own needs. By the time you have prayed for the other four groups, your own needs will be put into proper perspective.

The Ark of the Covenant

Exodus 25 describes God's directions in constructing the ark of the covenant. God gave directions to Moses when he was on Mount Sinai for forty days—the plans for the ark of the covenant. The ark measured 52x31x31 inches, was gilded with four rings of gold to the four poles, and had a golden-lidded (kaporet) mercy seat, with two golden cherubim. The ark contained the Ten Commandments, Aaron's rod, and a pot of manna. The Israelites would carry the ark into battle at all times, signifying God's presence and His protection. At the battle of Eben-Ezer, the Israelites were defeated by the Philistines, who stole the ark. Bad news travels fast.

Eli fell dead, and his daughter-in-law gave birth to a child who was called Ichabod—"the glory has departed." The ark was reclaimed in the defeat of Jericho. King David brought the ark back to Zion. He waited three months at the home of Obededom the Gittite, due to fact that one of the drivers of the cart was struck dead when he touched the ark.

During the construction of Solomon's temple, a special room

(Kodesh Hakodashim), Holy of Holies, was prepared to house the ark. King Hezekiah was the last person to view the ark. There is a present mystery today about the current location of the ark. Some say it was carried away by the Babylonians when they sacked Jerusalem, while still others say someone hid it in the Temple Mount.

Whatever happened to the ark of the covenant is not that important. What is important is that it was a symbol to God's people of the Old Testament of His divine presence and protection. Our God still utilizes the cherubim to be His messengers of protection for us.

My wife, Ruth, tells of a strange incident in a bookroom in Shanghai, China. She learned of it through her father, Dr. L. Nelson Bell, who served in the hospital in Tsingkiangpu, Kiangsu province. It was at this store that Dr. Bell bought his gospel portions and tracts to distribute among his patients.

The incident occurred in 1942, after the Japanese had won the war with China. One morning around nine o'clock, a Japanese truck stopped outside the bookroom. It was carrying five marines and was half-filled with books. The Christian Chinese shop assistant, who was alone at the time, realized with dismay that they had come to seize the stock. By nature timid, he felt this was more than he could endure.

Jumping from the truck, the marines made for the stop door; but before they could enter, a neatly dressed Chinese gentleman entered the shop ahead of them. Though the shop assistant knew practically all Chinese customers who traded there, this man was a complete stranger. For some unknown reason the soldiers seemed unable to follow him, and loitered about, looking in at the four large windows, but not entering. For two hours they stood around, until after eleven, but never set foot inside the door. The stranger asked what the men wanted, and the Chinese shop assistant explained that the Japanese were seizing stocks from many of the bookshops in the city, and now this store's turn had come, and so the two hours passed. At last the soldiers climbed into their army truck and drove away. The stranger also left, without making a single purchase or even inquiring about any times in the shop."

Later that day the shop owner, Mr. Christopher Willis, (whose Chinese name was Lee), returned. The shop assistant said to him, "Mr. Lee, do you believe in angels?" "I do" said Mr. Willis. "So do I, Mr. Lee." Could the stranger have been one of God's protecting angels? Dr. Bell always thought so.

CHAPTER SIX

HERALD OF COMMUNICATION

How do the angels communicate to human beings? Is it by the internet? Facebook? Instagram? Artificial intelligence? iPod? Television? Radio? Short wave? No! None of these methods! In the scriptures, angels revealed themselves to people in visions, dreams, and actual confrontation.

Let us study several of the accounts of angels communicating to God's people.

Zechariah

Zechariah had a vision one night of a man riding a red horse. He was standing among the myrtle trees in a ravine. Behind him were red, brown, and white horses. Zechariah asked the angel,

> "What is the meaning of this vision?" The angel answered, "I will show you what they are." Then the man standing among the myrtle trees explained, "They are the ones the Lord has sent to go throughout the earth." And they reported to the angel of the Lord, who was standing among

the myrtle trees, "We have gone throughout the whole world and found the whole world at rest and in peace." Then the angel of the Lord said, "Lord Almighty, how long will you withhold mercy from Jerusalem and from the towns of Judah, which you have been angry with these seventy years?" So the Lord spoke kind and comforting words to the angel who talked with me." (Zechariah 1:9–13)

In the following verses the Lord says that his house will be rebuilt and towns will overflow again with prosperity. God's holy messengers were sent to watch and to serve as communicating angels.

God communicates to us by means of his angels. Maybe we are not cognizant when they reveal themselves.

Moses

In his long speech before the Sanhedrin, Stephen relates the obdurate rebellion of the Israelites under Moses. While Moses was receiving the Ten Commandments, they formed an idol of a golden calf. Stephen concludes his speech in Acts 7:53: "You who have received the law that was put into effect through angels but have not obeyed it."

In Hebrews 2:2–3, the writer states, "For if the message spoken by angels was binding, and every violation and disobedience received its just punishment, how shall we escape if we ignore such a great salvation?"

We see how, even as Christians, we daily sin and disobey the Ten Commandments. But the world virtually ignores God, as if He doesn't exist. May we never ignore our God but always appreciate what God's angels do to communicate to us.

Balaam's Plan to Curse Israel

Balaam was a con artist from the get-go. His name, from the Hebrew, means "destruction." He was a mercenary who was authorized to curse Israel. The story begins when Balaam's donkey is quite stubborn and blocks the road three times. Three times, Balaam's beats his donkey to correct his behavior. The donkey stopped every time, for he saw an angel on the roadway.

Numbers aptly describes the situation:

> "Then the angel of the Lord stood in a narrow path between two vineyards, with walls on both sides. When the donkey saw the angel of the Lord, she pressed close to the wall, crushing Balaam's foot against it so he beat her again. Then the angel of the Lord moved on ahead and stood in a narrow place where there was no room to turn, either to the right or to the left. When the donkey saw the angel of the Lord, she lay down under Balaam, and he was angry and beat her with his staff." (Numbers 24:24–27)

In the remaining verses, Balaam negotiates with Balak to curse Israel, but instead, the curse was changed into a blessing. Every time he met with Balak, the mercenary built seven altars in order to denote completeness. God was with Balaam and stopped him in his tracks. Even though Balaam saw the angel in the road with a drawn sword, he continued with his plot. What was originally meant as a curse for God's people turned out to be a blessing.

Here, God's communicating angels were at work, and God had control of the situation. We can learn a lot from this story. First, we can see the hand of God, using his angels to communicate a message to people. Second, watch out for our stubbornness that at times sets us on a bad path of sin. Third, follow God's lead in our daily life.

Daniel

King Nebuchadnezzar had a detailed dream about a tree that none of the wise men of his court could interpret, but Daniel could.

Daniel 4:13–27 gives us a great interpretation of the king's dream. The tree represents Nebuchadnezzar, who had become great and strong and whose dominion extended to distant parts of the earth. The king would be drenched with dew, live with wild animals, and be driven away from people. This would occur seven times until he acknowledged and proclaimed that the Lord God is over all. In Daniel 4:28–37, the vision is fulfilled. The king's kingdom is restored, and Nebuchadnezzar exalts the King of heaven.

Here, we see how God works on the hearts of everyone, from the lowest to kings. God still operates quietly today and turns people from their sinful ways to serve the living Lord. God doesn't send dreams or visions but works through His Word. God's angels are messengers of His divine watchmen.

Philip and the Ethiopian

Acts 8:26–39 aptly describes the Ethiopian who was converted along the dusty trail. Let us search the scriptures.

> Now an angel of the Lord said to Philip, "Go south to the road––the desert road––to Gaza." So he started out, and on his way he met an Ethiopian eunuch, an important official in charge of all the treasury of Candace, queen of the Ethiopians. The man had gone to Jerusalem to worship, and on his way was sitting in his chariot reading the book of Isaiah the prophet. The Spirit told Philip, "Go to that chariot and stay near it." Then Philip ran up to the chariot and heard the man reading Isaiah the prophet. "Do you understand what you

are reading?" Philip asked. "How can I," he said,
"unless someone explains it to me?" So he invited
Philip to come up and sit with him." (Acts 8:26–31)

Philip observed that the Ethiopian was reading Isaiah 53:7–8.
The eunuch asked Philip who Isaiah was talking about. Philip then
proceeded to discuss the scripture with the man on a one-on-one
basis. When they passed some water, the man wanted to be baptized
by Philip. Philip baptized him.

Philip the apostle preached in Greece, Syria, and Phrygia.
Philip's name appears in several accounts in the Bible. They include
the following:

- He was a disciple of Jesus and from the city of Bethsaida.
- He was present when John the Baptist pointed out Jesus as
  the Lamb of God.
- He introduced Nathanael.
- He was present at the wedding at Cana.
- Philip suffered martyrdom at Hierapolis.

Symbols associated with the apostle include:

- The Latin cross
- The cross with two loaves of bread
- A spear with the patriarchal cross
- A cross with a carpenter's square

What do we learn about Philip's encounter with the man from
Ethiopia? Firsthand, we observe that Philip was very obedient to the
will of God. He easily could have taken a different road. We see that
he was on a mission—he spent time on a one-to-one basis with the
eunuch. What about us? Are we willing to be mission-minded and
spend time instructing people with the Word of God? The account
demonstrates how God used the angel to direct the apostle and to

both instruct and baptize him. The angel could not do that, but he could if directed by God's will. God uses us, as sinful as we are, to spread the good news of the gospel.

John was the only disciple who lived to a ripe old age without seeing martyrdom. He returned again to his hometown to preach the gospel. Angels are mentioned many times in the book of Revelation. At all times, we must appreciate the divine work that God's holy messengers do on our behalf. John states that all shall take place in the future.

Let us study the passages from the book of Revelation.

> Each of the four living creatures had six wings and was covered with eyes all around, even under their wings. Day and night they never stop saying: "Holy, holy, holy is the Lord God Almighty, who was, and is, and is to come." (Revelation 4:8)

> Then I looked and heard the voice of many angels, numbering thousands upon thousands and ten thousand times ten thousand. They encircled the throne and the living creatures and the elders. In a loud voice they sang: "Worthy is the Lamb, who was slain, to receive power and wealth and wisdom and strength and honor and glory and praise!" (Revelation 5:11–12)

> "All of the angels were standing around the throne and around the elders and the four living creatures. They fell down on their faces before the throne and worshiped God saying: Amen! Praise and glory and wisdom and thanks and honor and power and strength be to our God for ever and ever." Amen! (Revelation 7:11–12)

What do we learn from these three sections of the Bible?

- The angels praise God, twenty-four/seven.
- Christ is called the Lamb. (We sing a hymn in the Lutheran Church called "The Lamb.")
- Angels give all glory and honor to Christ.
- Angels worship Christ.

What about our worship life? Do we praise God in adverse times as well as in good times? Has church attendance in our congregations increased over the years? Do we honor and praise God at all times?

Cornelius

> At Caesarea there was a man named Cornelius, a centurion in what was known as the Italian Regiment. He and his family were devout and God-fearing; he gave generously to those in need and prayed to God regularly. One day at about three in the afternoon he had a vision. He distinctly saw an angel of God, who came to him and said, "Cornelius!" Cornelius stared at him in fear. "What is it, Lord?" he asked. The angel answered, "Your prayers and gifts to the poor have come up before God. "Now send men to Joppa to bring back a man named Simon who is called Peter. He is staying with Simon the tanner, whose house is by the sea." When the angel who spoke to him had gone, Cornelius called two of his servants and one of his soldiers who was a devout man. He told them everything that had happened and sent them to Joppa." (Acts 10:1–8)

During my tour of the Holy Land in 2011, our group visited Joppa, which is a port city. As you arrive you see a large statue of Peter greeting you. It is now highly commercialized with gift shops along the waterfront, which really detracts from Joppa.

What can we learn from this story about Cornelius?

He was not only a Centurion with one hundred men under his command, but he also was a proselyte of the Temple Gate. God was using him, a man of Jewish faith, to bring the gospel to the Gentiles. God uses all of us when we use our spiritual gifts for the kingdom of God. That is why we should avail ourselves to take the Houts Questionnaire on spiritual gifts in order to discover and use our gifts for our Lord. Are you using your spiritual gifts for Christ?

Acts 10:9–16 describes Peter's vision to discipline him that the gospel is not only for the Jews but for the Gentiles.

John's Revelation

John was banished to the island of Patmos during the persecutions of the time. I was on the island of Patmos twice—in 2010 and in 2012. On both occasions, I walked down the steps to the dimly lit grotto where John, by verbal inspiration, penned God's Word. One block from the approach to the grotto is a museum, tended by monks, that houses important artifacts.

> The revelation of Jesus Christ, which God gave him to show his servants what must take place. He made it known by sending his angel to his servant John, who testifies to everything he saw-that is, the word of God and the testimony of Jesus Christ, Blessed is the one who reads the words of this prophecy, and blessed are those who hear it and and take to heart what is written in it, because the time is near. (Revelation 1:1–3)

CHAPTER SEVEN

HERALD OF DEATH

Cryonics

Death is inevitable! God never wanted man to die. God's desire was that Adam and Eve would live in the garden of Eden forever. Due to man's disobedience, sin plunged the human race into spiritual depravity. God planned a solution—the promise of a Savior to save the world from sin, death, and the power of Satan. The scriptures declare. "The wages of sin is death, but the gift of God is eternal life through Jesus Christ our Lord" (Romans 6:23).

In Ezekiel 18:4, the prophet states, "The soul who sins is the one who will die."

Humankind tenaciously promulgates cryonics—freezing the body of a person who has died of a disease, hoping to restore life when a cure for the disease is found. Phoenix, Arizona, and other large cities in the United States have such facilities to freeze bodies. Ted Williams's body is hovering in suspension in cryonics. Bodies are place in cylinders, which are labeled with their names, dates of death, and causes of death. Humankind constantly clings to the false notion that these bodies, when thawed out, will be brought to life. Utter foolishness! Yet loved ones will pay exorbitant costs to do this for their loved ones. Scripturally, it is wrong. No one can bring a person back to life, and scientifically, different parts of the body thaw out at different intervals. When thawed, the bodies will be mush, and the soul is gone from the body at death.

An Evangelist Defeat

Years ago, an evangelist in Arkansas attempted to thaw out the body of his mother. The body had been frozen and displayed before his congregation on a daily basis. Through his many intercessions, he was unable to revive the body of his mother. Don't people read and know the scriptures?

Reincarnation

Reincarnation is a fallacy that has floated around the world for a long time. They say that when a person dies, that person returns to the earth as something different. At my large parish in Michigan, I witnessed a tragic auto accident on the road of my church. The person died. People swarmed to the tragic scene, but it was most tragic that a Hindu person, who believed in reincarnation, rushed to the dead body. Here again, people have a wrong concept of death and the afterlife.

COVID-19

During 2020–22, the world was faced with the devastating blow of COVID-19, especially with the delta and omicron variants. Doctors said that if people were vaccinated and had the booster shot, it could keep them out of the hospital. People throughout the world are obdurate and foolish in not being vaccinated.

The Rich Man and Lazarus

In Luke 16:19–31, we have the account that Jesus told during his ministry on this earth. The rich man had everything in this life.

Poor Lazarus had a difficult time keeping body and soul together. The rich man went to hell due to his unbelief, while Lazarus went to heaven by his faith. In hell, the rich man called out to send Abraham and Lazarus to his five brothers in order that they would avert hell.

> He said to him, "If they do not listen to Moses and the Prophets, they will not be convinced even if someone rises from the dead." (Luke 16:31)

Those in heaven are in bliss, while those in hell are in torment.

Sodom and Gomorrah

In Genesis 19:1–26, we have the account of two angels visiting Lot at the gateway of the city. They had a divine mission in mind—to avenge God's people and spare their lives. The men of Sodom had seen that the two angels were men, and they lusted after them. At first, Lot offered his two daughters, but no, they wanted the men. The men of Sodom pushed Lot out of the way and threatened to break down the door. Immediately, the two avenging angels sprang into action by blinding the men and protecting Lot and his family. Lot warned his sons-in-law to flee with their wives and Lot's family, but they thought that he was joking. The angels told Lot to hurry and flee for their lives! They did allow Lot to flee to the next town, which was Zoar. They were all instructed to flee and not to look back at the destruction of Sodom and Gomorrah. Genesis 19:26 says, "Lot's wife looked back and she became a pillar of salt." That is why at every mealtime in our household, I say "Please pass me Lot's wife."

In this story, we see God's mighty angels bringing death and destruction to Sodom and Gomorrah and also protecting Lot and his daughters. What about today? Does our gracious Lord rescue us from harm and danger? He may not take away the danger, but He gives us the strength to carry on every day. When was the most recent time you found yourself in a very difficult situation? Did you call upon the name of the Lord? Or did you, as so many other people choose to do, keep a stiff upper lip and think, *I will be tough and sail right through this mess.*

Don't follow the lead of this world. The world will lead you astray.

The Christian views death entirely differently from the world. To the world, when you die, that is the total end. For the Christian, we will inherit eternal life by faith in Christ as our personal Savior. In the great chapter on the Resurrection, Paul states,

> "O death, where is your sting? O grave, where is your victory? The sting of death is sin; and the strength of sin is the law. But thanks be to God, which gives us the victory through our Lord Jesus Christ." (1 Corinthians 15:55)

Paul also says, "For to me is Christ, and to die is gain" (Philippians 1:21).

Upon death, the angels of God usher the soul of the believer into the presence of God in heaven.

All humankind will endure temporal death—the separation of the soul from the body. Death comes to all ages. Too many people surmise that death chiefly comes to old people. That is not true. I have officiated at hundreds of funerals in my ministry, and many were young people.

For when you eat of it you will surely die. (Genesis 2:17)

Death is depicted three ways: (1) spiritual death—the separation of the soul from God, (2) temporal death—the separation of the soul from the body, and (3) eternal death—the separation of both body and soul from God.

The term *second death* is recorded in the book of Revelation 2:11; 20:6, 14; 21:8. The apostle John, under divine inspiration, says that those who overcome the devil's tribulation are holy. They have a part in the first resurrection and will not experience the second death. Believers are not subject to the second death. They only die a temporal death. Unbelievers will have two deaths, temporal and spiritual death.

What Is Your Sign?

At a Religious Emphasis Week on a university campus, the students were studying their horoscopes in order to determine under what sign they were born. Some said "Cancer," while others said "Capricorn." But one Christian student said, "I am a Christian and born under the sign of the cross." What a great witness this young student made to the other students!

The Angel Strikes

King Sennacherib, king of Assyria, threatened to destroy Jerusalem. He tried to con good king Hezekiah to make a bargain—that Sennacherib would give Jerusalem two thousand horses if Hezekiah surrendered to him. Repeatedly, Hezekiah said no, and he turned to the Lord in prayer, stating that Sennacherib defied the name of God and asked the Lord that the king of Assyria be defeated. Hezekiah and his court sat in sackcloth and tore their clothing. Isaiah appeared and notified the good king that there was nothing to fear. Isaiah, in a long portion of 2 Kings 19, foretells the end of Sennacherib and his army.

> That night the angel of the Lord went out and put to death a hundred and eighty-five thousand men in the camp. When the people got up the next morning- there were all dead bodies. (2 Kings 19:35–36)

Sennacherib returned to Nineveh, where two of his sons killed him. This was all prophesied by Hezekiah, whose name, from the Hebrew, means "the strength of the Lord."

How did this one angel accomplish this great feat? Did God use pestilence, a plague, or another army to kill the 185,000 men? We will never know. That is not the most important item. The most important item was that God's angel of death defeated the enemy and that Hezekiah's prayer was answered.

What about us? Do we rely upon God's strength and power at all times? I hope we do.

Paul states, "I can do everything through him who gives me strength" (Philippians 4:13).

The Death Knell

What happens as death strikes? In this lifetime, humans are a total personality of body and soul. At the point of death, the soul is separated from the body. The souls of believers are ushered into the presence of God by angels, while the souls of unbelievers go to hell. Bodies are buried or cremated, awaiting the Day of Resurrection, when all of the bodies of all people in all parts of the world will be raised. The glorified bodies of believers will be reunited with their souls in heaven, while the bodies of unbelievers will be reunited with their souls in hell. Death, for the Christian, is depicted as falling asleep in this lifetime and awakening in heaven.

> I will lie down and sleep in peace, for you alone, O
> Lord, make me dwell in safety. (Psalm 4:8)

The Saints

> To live above with saints we love,
> Lord, that will be grace and glory;
> To live below with saints we know:
> Wow! that's another story!

Herod Agrippa I

Acts 12:21–23 depicts the folly and blasphemy of Herod Agrippa I. He, like other rulers, thought he was a god.

> [The people] shouted, "This is the voice of a god, not of a man." (Acts 12:22)

An angel of God struck Herod, and he was eaten by worms and died. Herod was the son of Aristobulus and became ruler upon the death of his uncle Herod Philip II. Herod was given the title of king by Caligula. Herod persecuted the Christians of the first century, but in spite of him and other wicked rulers, the gospel was spread to the far corners of the world. We see the mighty hand of God moving with the angel who killed Herod and afflicted him with a disease that consumed his body with worms. Our God will not allow the heathen to make mockery of Him but will proceed to bring destruction upon the wicked. God's angel sent a terrible, agonizing death to Herod Agrippa I.

Bunco Squad

Bunco squad is an informal name given to the law enforcement department in major US cities that tracks fraud cases. They ferret out the insidious charlatans who, by different means, scam people.

Séances and spiritualism became popular in the mid-nineteenth century. Spiritualists or mediums attempted to communicate with the dead or promised great success to people. One medium in New Orleans during the 1880s was especially successful and became very wealthy. What she predicted came to fruition. How did she do it? What magical powers did she have? In the 1900s, scientists looked into this case and discovered why she was successful. During the day, she operated a hair salon for women. She would probe and gather information from the women, which she then used as a medium at night. When she found out that the boss of one client had an extramarital affair, she blackmailed him so that her client received a promotion. Mary Todd Lincoln had a séance upon the death of her son Willie.

It is impossible to communicate with the dead. These mediums are frauds and charlatans. Those who have died do not have any communication with those on the earth. The souls of believers enjoy the bliss of heaven while the unbelievers are in hell. We on this earth cannot communicate with the dead.

CHAPTER EIGHT

HERALD OF JUDGMENT

Angels play an integral role in judgment. Let us study how angels deal with humankind. Different religious sects have tried to determine the exact day and hour that our Lord Jesus will return to judge the living and the dead in His parous? No one knows God's secret hour.

> No one knows that day or hour, not even the angels in heaven, nor the Son, but only the Father. (Matthew 24:36)

The early Christians had a good grasp of eschatology (the final events of the world or humankind), for they said Jesus died yesterday, rose today, and will come again tomorrow.

Obdurate People

We are living in an age of gross spiritual darkness, indifference, and obdurate hearts. People casually toss off the notion of heaven and hell. Some say that if God is so gracious, how can He ever send a person to hell? They fail to realize the full category of God's divine attributes. He condemns sin and punishes impenitent sinners. Just think of the glory and bliss that awaits us Christians in heaven when we see a Luther, a Matthew, other greats of God, and our loved ones in heaven—joy beyond comprehension!

Jesus's Lament over Jerusalem

Jesus said,

> "O Jerusalem, Jerusalem, you who kill the prophets and stone those sent to you, how often I have longed to gather your children together, as a hen gathers your chicks under her wings, but you are not willing. Look, your house is left to you desolate. For I tell you, you will not see me again until you say, 'Blessed is he who comes in the name of the Lord.'" (Matthew 23:37–39)

The people in Jesus's day, as in our day, had spiritual blinders on and failed to acknowledge the impending demise of Jerusalem, especially the temple.

> "Do you see all these great buildings?" replied Jesus. "Not one stone here will be left on another; every one will be thrown down." (Mark 13:2)

St. Francis Dam

The St. Francis Dam was built from 1924 to 1926 to serve the water requirements of Los Angeles. When the dam failed in 1928, 431 lives were lost. The chief engineer of this project was William Mulholland, who had received accolades for construction of the Los Angeles Aqueduct in 1913.

Why did the dam fail? There were several reasons:

- Defective soil foundation
- Built too high
- Dam tilting

The question is, how many of those people who died in disaster knew Jesus Christ as their personal Lord and Savior? For those who had accepted Christ, their souls were ushered to heaven by angels.

We confess in the Christian creeds regarding Judgment Day, "He will come to judge the living and the dead." What a grand scene that will be for Christians on Judgment Day. The Christians still alive at Christ's return will be united with their souls in heaven. In heaven, they will enjoy a glorified body with their souls. It will be just the opposite for unbelievers. Their bodies will be cast to hell eternally, where their souls were already at death.

Actually, the place of our future in eternity occurs when our souls are separated from the bodies. For the Christian, angels—God's messengers at our deaths—take our souls to heaven.

Personal Guardian Angels

Does every child of God have a personal guardian angel to watch over him or her, twenty-four/seven? No. This would be a good subject to pursue for a doctorate in sacred theology (STD). We wish we had a guardian angel, but the Bible does not state this. Guardian angels watch over Christians in their everyday lives, but to say we each have a personal guardian angel is a far stretch and not biblical. When we travel, we do ask the Lord to send His angels to watch over and protect us from every evil.

Signs of the End of the World

Today, in 2023, we see signals sent from heaven by God of the early prelude to Judgment Day. Recently, we have more worldwide floods, rumors of war, more disasters, indifference and much more. These items are a prelude to the Last Day.

> "Nation will rise against nation, and kingdom against kingdom. There will be famines and earthquakes in various places. All these are the beginning of birth pains. Then you will be handed over to be persecuted and put to death, and you will be hated by all nations because of me. At that time many will turn away from the faith and will betray and hate each other, and many false prophets will appear and deceive many people. Because of the increase of wickedness, the love of most will grow cold, but he who stands firm to the end will be saved. And this gospel of the kingdom will be preached in the whole world as a testimony to all nations, and then the end will come." (Matthew 24:7–14)

> At that time the sign of the Son of Man will appear in the sky, and all nations of the earth will mourn. They will see the Son of Man coming on the clouds of the sky, with power and great glory. And he will send his angels with a loud trumpet call, and they will gather his elect from the four winds, from one end of the heavens to the other. (Matthew 24:30–31)

Just think! The trumpet blast will be heard around the world when Christ returns on Judgment Day!

The Parable of the Ten Virgins

Jesus, in His earthly ministry, delivered the message of the kingdom of God (Greek: *basileia tou theou*). Our Savior taught in parables, not only to His disciples but to the crowds that followed him. A parable is an earth story that tells a spiritual truth. There is only one point of comparison (*tertium comparationis*). In Matthew 25, Jesus uses three parables to prepare the people for His future, impending return on Judgment Day. Matthew 25:1–13 tells the story of the ten virgins. Marriages in New Testament times were great celebrations that lasted several days. In our present day, weddings and the receptions are over by midnight. In New Testament times, there was a longer period of preparation.

There were five wise and five foolish virgins. The foolish ones failed to have enough oil in their lamps, while the wise were fully prepared. The bridegroom was detained, and all ten fell asleep. "At midnight the cry rang out: "Here's the bridegroom! Come out, to meet him!"[19] (Matthew 25:6). All of the ten women checked the oil in their lamps. The five wise virgins had enough oil for their lamps, while the five foolish women were deficient. The foolish virgins asked the wise women for oil. They refused, advising them to go out and buy oil. While the five foolish virgins were gone, the bridegroom arrived. The foolish women came back, trying to get in. The door was shut.

> "Therefore keep watch, because you do not know
> the day or the hour." (Matthew 25:13)

The number ten denote completeness. Ten is recorded in the Bible several times. Ten is the number required to establish a synagogue. The five wise virgins had their lamps burning, full of oil, when the bridegroom arrived. The oil is a symbol of the Holy Spirit

---

[19] From the Greek, Exerchomai, "come out", William and Robert Mounce, Greek and English Interlinear New Testament (Zondervan, 2008).

or the graces of God. At the beginning of their vigil, all were ready. The unwise took no effort to keep their spiritual lives healthy. The bridegroom in the parable is Christ. In the scriptures, the church is recorded as the bride of Jesus, the divine bridegroom, who will come again suddenly. The key word is *watch*—be on the alert. Always be prepared for Christ's Second Advent, when He will come with His angels. What about us today? Are we wise or foolish believers? Do we keep our light of faith aglow as we await the coming of our Lord? *Watch!*

The Parable of the Talents

Matthew 25:14–30 tells the parable of the talents. This inspired vignette begins when a man goes on a trip and leaves not only instructions but a lesson about his property. To one, he gave five talents, to another two talents, and to the other one talent. All were supposed to invest the money. A talent is five hundred dollars in our currency today; in Jesus's day, that amount was a fortune. The man with five talents invested his money and earned five additional talents. The man who received two talents also invested his money, and he doubled his investment. The third man, thinking that his master was difficult, hid his talent. The master commended the man with the five talents and the man with the two talents. The master condemned and punished the man who hid his one talent. This shows the fidelity of the two and the lack of trust of one. The man who received only one talent and failed to invest it used excuses to justify his lack of action.

> "Then the man who had received the one talent came, 'Master, he said 'I knew that you are a hard man, harvesting where you have not sown and gathering where you have not scattered seed." (Matthew 25:24)

95

This is a saying that denotes a desire to obtain results without sufficient means. The Greek word is *diaskorpizo*.[20]

In order to avoid tautology, *winnowing* is the correct interpretation. The Hebrew word is *zarah*, signifying gathering corn from a floor where you winnow.

Jesus wants to point out that all talents, great or small, must be used in His service. Whether the return is large or small, it shows a whiling mind and real faithfulness. When we appear before the eternal judge on Judgment Day, we cannot claim we didn't know our Lord's will, and we can't make up excuses. Jesus requires faithfulness from Christians. How faithful are you? Many people were baptized and confirmed as teenagers. Have you been faithful to the vow you made at God's altar on the day of your confirmation?

> Well done, good and faithful servant, you have been faithful over a few things, I will put you in charge of many things. Come and share your master's happiness. (Matthew 25:23)

> Be faithful, even to the point of death, and I will give you the crown of life. (Revelation 2:10b)

The Olympics of ancient times, usually held in Athens, Greece, awarded the winner of a race a crown made of leaves that had withered and died. The crown of life that God gives to His faithful Christians is the crown of eternal life in heaven, which will be forever.

---

[20]   Diaskorpizo, Greek for "to scatter abroad"; scatter in Matthew 25:24, W. E. Vine, Vines' Expository Dictionary of Old and New Testament Words (Nashville: Thomas Nelson Publishers. 1997), 997.

The Sheep and the Goats

In many of Jesus's discourses, He used parables to better communicate the meaning of the kingdom of God. The Eastern mind, different from the Western mind, is drawn to word pictures instead of concrete terms. Matthew 25:31–46 records the parable of the sheep and the goats.

> When the Son of Man comes in his glory, and all the angels with him, he will sit on his throne in heavenly glory. (Matthew 25:31)

The story relates that Christ will separate the sheep (believers) from the goats (unbelievers) on the Day of Judgment. Jesus, as the King of kings and Lord of lords, separates the two on the basis of what they accomplished while on the earth. Jesus uses terms such as, *when I was hungry, I was thirsty, I was a stranger,* and *I needed clothes,* and *I was sick.* The righteous were unaware what they had done. Jesus commanded them.

Some churches interpret this section of the scriptures as proving that a person is saved by good works. This text reveals just the opposite of that teaching; it shows that by faith, Christians did these things. It was not to save themselves but purely to show that good works are the fruit of faith.

Matthew 25:34 is clear:

> Then the King will say to those on his right, "Come, you who are blessed by my Father; take your inheritance, the kingdom prepared for you since the creation of the world."

Nota bene: Jesus used the word *inheritance*.[21] An inheritance is an item you receive as a gift in the last will and testament of a loved one. You have not earned it, but it has been given to you as a gift. We may never receive an earthly inheritance, but we are guaranteed by our Lord that we will receive an eternal inheritance in heaven through the merits of Jesus Christ, our Lord.

Paul, the apostle, reminds us, "Giving thanks to the Father, who has qualified you to share in the inheritance of the saints in the kingdom of light" (Colossians 1:12).

Passover

Jehovah had sent nine of the ten plagues to Egypt, but Pharaoh would not relent to let the Israelites leave Egypt. The tenth plague that was sent would kill the firstborn, and there would not be a successor to the throne.

> This is what the Lord says: "About midnight I will go throughout Egypt. Every firstborn son in Egypt will die, from the firstborn son of Pharaoh, who sits on the throne, to the firstborn of the slave girl, who is at he hand mill, and all the firstborn of the cattle as well. There will be a loud wailing throughout Egypt-worse than there has ever been or ever will be again." (Exodus 11:4–6)

Then, it happened. All of the firstborn died.

Before this plague took place, God directed the Israelites to mark with lamb's blood above their doors in order that Yahweh would pass over them, and they would be spared the death of their

---

21   Kieronomeo, Greek for "inheritance; to receive as one's own, to obtain." W.E. Vine, Vines's Expository Dictionary of Old & New Testament Words (Nashville: Thomas Nelson Publishers, 1997), 588.

firstborns. At midnight when the Angel of Death passed over, God's people would be saved by the blood of the lamb.

Passover (Hebrew: *Pesach*) is observed in the Holy Land for seven days and celebrated by Jews throughout the world. *Chametz*—leaven—is forbidden for the Passover. There is even a blessing for a search to eliminate and remove all chametz before the Passover begins.

On the first night of Passover, they sit down at a seder (the Hebrew word for order or arrangement). The Haggadah retells the experiences in Egypt and is read while four cups of wine are drunk. The Haggadah is divided into fifteen parts:

1. Kadeish—recital of kiddush and drinking the first cup of wine
2. Urchatz—the washing of the hands
3. Karpas—dipping the karpas in salt water
4. Yachatz—breaking the middle matzo
5. Maggid—retelling the Passover story and telling the four questions while the second cup of wine is drunk
6. Rachtzah—second washing of hands
7. Motzi-Motsiy—blessings before eating bread products
8. Matzo Maso—blessing before eating matzo
9. Maror—eating of the maror
10. Koreich Korekh—eating of a sandwich made of matzo and maror
11. Shulchan oreich—the serving of the meal
12. Tzafun Tsafun Safun—eating of the afikomen.
13. Bareich Barekhn—meal blessing and consuming of third cup of wine
14. Hallel—drinking of the fourth cup of wine
15. Nirtzah Niyr-tsah Niyr-sah—conclusion

The maror are bitter herbs to symbolize the bitterness of slavery in Egypt.

The afikomen is used to arouse the interest of the children at the seder meal. The leader breaks the matzo into two in order to keep the children awake, and by hiding the afikomen, the children can win a prize when it is found. ("Passover," Wikipedia)

My Ministry Experiences

I have been in the ministry of the Lutheran Church for sixty-four years, and I have witnessed needy cases on several occasions. When I was in Troy, New York, many beggars came to our door. I would not give them money, but my wife prepared sandwiches that they ate on our back porch. When I was in Chicago in an inner-city congregation, there were many hard-luck stories. One family said they needed money to buy cough medicine for their child. I told them that I had an account at Osco Drugstore. I told them to go there, give their name, and mention my account, and they would receive the meds. The family did not go to the drugstore.

Judgment at Nuremberg

Near the end of World War II, the German army knew that they were losing. Many skipped off to South America and assumed new identities. Many of them had surreptitiously squirreled away stolen art that they had taken from Jews. But these Nazis were not safe, for after the war, a special group called Mossad[22] hunted down these killers in order to bring them to justice. The squad found the killers in South America, but at that time, South American countries would not issue extradition papers.

The team observed the Nazis, kidnapped and drugged them, and got them on a plane to Germany. The Nuremberg trials were held from November 20, 1945, to October 1, 1946. The court desired to convict twenty-four of the political and military leaders of the Third

---

[22]   Mossad, the national intelligence agency of Israel that captured and brought to justice Nazi war criminals. It was organized December 13, 1949, with the motto from Proverbs 11:14: "For lack of guidance a nation falls, but many advisors make victory sure." St. L. VII: 1480f.

Reich. The first trial was conducted by the International Military Tribunal. Lesser war criminals were tried at the US Nuremberg Military Tribunal. The Nuremberg trials included genocide, war crimes, extermination of racial and national groups, and the destruction of the territories of the Jews, Poles, and Gypsies. Most of the Nazis received the death sentence, some life sentences, and a few were acquitted. Death would be by hanging. Hermann Goring, Martin Bormann, Hans Frank, Alfred Jodl, Ernst Kaltenbrunner, Wilhelm Keitel, Joachim von Ribbentrop, Alfred Rosenberg, Fritz Sauckel, Arthur Seyss-Inquart, Alfred Speer, and Julius Streicher received the death penalty. Rudolf Hess was imprisoned for life. The court revealed the great atrocities that the Nazis had committed during the war. Only eternity will reveal if any of these Nazis repented of their gross sins.

What about us today? No, we would never be accused of such crimes or face a prison sentence, but daily, we must repent of our sins and seek forgiveness through the blood of Jesus Christ, our Lord.

Adolf Eichmann was captured by the Mossad agents in Argentina on May 11, 1960, found guilty of war crimes, and hanged in 1962.

1 Thessalonians 4:13–18

What do we know about Thessalonica? Paul received a vision that cried, "Come over to Macedonia and help us," This was Paul's Macedonian call to bring the gospel to Europe. Paul came to Thessalonica on his second missionary journey. The city was named after Alexander the Great's half-sister. Thessalonica was a city of 200,000. As a chief harbor town, trade poured into the city.

In 2012, I hosted a tour to Greece, and we visited Thessalonica. We arrived at their small airport, and all of the other passengers' luggage was accounted for—but not ours. Finally, the one carousal was restarted, and we received our luggage. The time was 7:00 p.m., and we had a two-hour bus ride to the next town for lodging. Thessalonica of today is large with a population of several million.

We discussed many of the signs of the coming of Day of Wrath. We must always be watchful. Protestant Reformer Martin Luther wrote,

> Heaven and earth will creak and crack and act in every way as ready to crash and collapse and act in every way as though they divined that the world is soon to come to an end and that The Day is close at hand.

In 1 Thessalonians, Paul reminded the members that the Lord will come as a thief in the night, and he urged watchfulness. But this produced an unhealthy situation, where the people had stopped working and had abandoned all ordinary pursuits to await the Second Coming. They worried over what would happen to those who died before the Second Coming arrived.

Paul said, "Or to grieve like the rest of men, who have no hope" (1 Thessalonians 4:13). When our loved ones die, it is normal to have a satisfactory time of grieving. But to grieve for years is not good for our physical lives or spiritual lives. Closure is important. As Christians, we have an eschatological assurance that we will have a joyous reunion with our loved ones in heaven.

> We believe that Jesus died and rose again and so we believe that God will bring with Jesus those who have fallen asleep in him. (1 Thessalonians 4:14)

As we are with our sin, iniquities, and putrefactions, we cannot stand before the Lord.

> And the blood of Jesus, his Son, purifies us from all sin. (1 John 1:7b)

> Because I live, you shall live also. (John 14:19)

St. Paul is the crème de la crème of the apostles. He states,

> According to the Lord's own word, we tell you that
> we who are still alive, who are left till the coming
> of the Lord, will not precede[23] those who have fallen
> asleep. (1 Thessalonians 4:15)

The early Christians at Thessalonica thought that the living
would have a preference over the dead. Paul assures them that the
dead in Christ shall rise first.

> For the Lord himself will come down from heaven,
> with a loud command[24] with the voice of the
> archangel and with the trumpet call of God, and
> the dead in Christ will rise first. Paul stated that the
> dead shall rise first and those who will be living will
> be reunited with those who died. They shall ever
> be with the Lord. We await the great reveille of the
> sound of the trumpet.
> After that, we who are still alive and are left,
> will be caught up[25] with them in the clouds to meet
> the Lord in the air. And so we will be with the Lord
> forever. (1 Thessalonians 4:16–17)

Some churches teach the Rapture, but the Rapture is contrary
to the scriptures and is false doctrine. Paul is speaking about the
Resurrection and not a secret return of Christ.

> Therefore encourage[26] each other with these words.
> (1 Thessalonians 4:18)

---

[23] Phthano, Greek for "to come sooner than expected".
[24] Kelensmati, Greek for "field command".
[25] Harpazo, Greek for "snatched away".
[26] Parakaleite, Greek for "comfort".

These are words from Paul to strengthen the faith of this congregation and to reassure them of the joyous reunion with their loved ones in heaven.

Pompeii

Pompeii was a harbor town and was noted for its sexual immorality. I saw the ruins of Pompeii on the tour to this city. Pompeii was destroyed by the burning ash when Mount Vesuvius erupted. Some bodies were found in the streets as they were attempting to flee; some were found in deep vaults, as if they had gone there for security. But where did they find the Roman sentinels? They found them standing at the city gates with their hands grasping their weapons. While the searing ash engulfed them and burned them to cinders, they stood guard at their posts. So let us be found ever watchful and always prepared for the end.

Maranatha––our Lord, come!

CHAPTER NINE

HERALDS—PAST, PRESENT, FUTURE

Heralds of the Past

A herald is a proclaimer or messenger of news. The Old Testament has references to these proclaimers. They are noted in Psalm 40:9; Isaiah 61:1; Nehemiah 5:7; Jonah 3:2: Leviticus 23:24; 25:9; and Daniel 3:4.

In the New Testament, we see them in 1 Timothy 2:7; 2 Timothy 1:11; 2 Peter 2:5; John 1:19–33; and 1 Corinthians 9:27.

Missionaries of the past certainly obeyed the command of our Lord Jesus in the great commission.

> Then Jesus came to them and said, "All authority in heaven and on earth has been given to me. Therefore go and make disciples of all nations, baptizing them in the name of the Father and of the Son and of the Holy Spirit, and teaching them to obey everything I have commanded you. And surely I will be with you always, to the very end of the age." (Matthew 28:18–20)

Throughout the numerous decades, many missionaries have devoted themselves inexhaustibly to the growth of God's kingdom. I will name just a few. On the mission field of China, there was Dr. L. Nelson Bell (father-in-law to Billy Graham) and A. A. Talbot. In India, there was Adoniram Judson. The New Hebrides Islands had John Gibson Paton and John Geddie. In retrospect, we must highlight the work of the apostle Paul, who turned the world upside down on his missionary sojourns around the world as the messenger to the Gentiles. We must also note the eleven disciples who served their Lord faithfully. Ten suffered martyrdom, while John died a natural death.

Coming closer to home in the United States, we had Dr. Billy Graham, founder of his crusades in many cities. My wife and I attended one of his crusades in 1996 when we were in Louisville, Kentucky. He preached a Christ-centered message! There were other evangelists also. Among them are the following:

1. Dwight L. Moody, founder of the Moody Church in Chicago. He started the Moody Bible Institute in Chicago.
2. Billy Sunday, who played Major League baseball for eight years and became famous in many cities with his evangelistic rallies.
3. William Booth was the founder of the Salvation Army in 1878. His roots were from London, England.
4. Charles E. Fuller became a Baptist pastor in 1925. He is well known as the host of *The Old-Fashioned Revival Hour*. ABC picked up his program on 650 stations in 1951. He founded Fuller Theological Seminary in Pasadena, California, in 1947.
5. John the Baptist, was a harbinger of Christ, preparing the way for Christ.

Present

Not too much is recorded about present-day missionaries. When I graduated from Concordia Seminary in 1958, five men were sent to the mission field. The seminary trained them many months for their call. They accepted the Macedonian call, as did Paul.

Franklin Graham, son of Dr. Billy Graham, assumed his father's position in the Billy Graham campaign upon the death of his father.

There are probably many more present-day missionaries of all denominations who are the unsung heroes of the faith. They are recorded only upon the death of the missionary.

"From Greenland's Icy Mountain"

Reginald Heber penned this hymn in 1819. He was a genius. At the age of seven, he was translating classic Latin to English, and at seventeen, he was enrolled at Oxford. He served sixteen years as the pastor of a church in Shrewsbury, England. He wrote fifty-seven hymns during his lifetime. He died of a stroke in 1826.

> From Greenland's icy mountains,
> From India's coral strand,
> Where Afric's sunny fountains
> Roll down their golden sand,
> From many an ancient river,
> From many a palmy plain,
> They call us to deliver
> Their land from error's chain.[27]

---

[27] Worship and Service Hymnal: For Church, School, and Home, Hymnary. org, #431.

Future

The seven letters to the churches of Asia Minor are timely for past, present, and future. What is meant by "angels" in the book of Revelation? Some state they are messengers sent by the churches to John on Patmos, while others state they are the pastors or guardian angels of the churches. Two churches, Smyrna and Philadelphia, are all praise, while in Sardis and Laodicea, it is all blame. With the other three—Pergamum, Thyatira, and Ephesus—there is a mixture of both praise and blame.

What is the future of Christianity? What is the future of denominationalism? Statisticians reveal in their records the following:

1. People distrust institutions, such as the government.
2. Distrust in denominations is due to scandals, social issues, and sexual harassment by leaders.
3. Millennials are waiting until thirty to get married.
4. There is a rise in secularism.
5. In 1975, 68 percent of the population embraced Christianity, while in 2002, it dropped to 36 percent.[28]
6. In the Silent Generation (1928–1945), 84 percent claim Christianity; Boomers—76 percent; Millennials—29; four in ten are religious nuns, and one in ten Millennials is of non-Christian faiths.[29]

These statistics spin a dismal outlook for the church at large. What do you think concerning this subject?

Throughout the ages, the church has contended with persecution, martyrdom, apostasy, false doctrine, unfaithfulness, competition with the world, narcissism, and a lot more. The church has always come back as the victor. Listen to Jesus's words to Peter:

---

[28] Frank Newport, "Why Are Americans Losing Confidence in Organize Religion?" Gallup.

[29] Pew Research Center, 2019.

"And I tell you that you are Peter, and on this rock
I will build my church, and the gates of Hades will
not overcome it." (Matthew 16:18)

In Greek, *Peter* is derived from *petros*, meaning rock. Some
churches advocate that Christ desired to build His church upon
Peter, as a man. This is wrong. The church will be built upon the
rock faith of believers, as was Peter.

Sure, there will be church mergers, and some congregations will
close, but the church at large *moves forward*!

What is the student enrollment at the denominational churches?
All have declining numbers, and the numbers decline seriously
every year. The Lutheran Church–Missouri Synod maintains two
seminaries: St. Louis, and Fort Wayne, Indiana. When I graduated
sixty-four years ago from Concordia Seminary, there were 220 in
my class (the highest class number on record). In 2021, there was a
total of 443 in both seminaries combined.

What has happened? Is it a lack of dedication from young men?
No. Is it the lack of prayers by families for their sons? No. What,
then, are the causes?

1. Lack of recruitment
2. Lack of congregational support
3. High cost of training
4. The lure of industry that offers better pay and higher degrees

The Lutheran church is planning to pay for the tuition of
aspiring seminarians.

CHAPTER TEN

ANGEL OF THE LORD

The angel of the Lord is a theophany, a manifestation of God before Christ's preincarnation. This term only appears in the Old Testament, not in the New Testament.

Jesus, in His earthly ministry, had many encounters with the Pharisees, who were a self-righteous group who believed that for every bone in the human body, they had a law that they thought they could keep. We have such an encounter in John:

> "You are not yet fifty years old," the Jews said to him, "and you have seen Abraham!"
>
> "I tell you the truth," Jesus answered, "before Abraham was born, I am!" These words angered them and they tried to stone him. (John 8:57–58)

Let us look at some of the examples from the Old Testament that denote the angel of the Lord.

Abraham and Isaac

In the account in Genesis 22:1–18. God severely tested Abraham, but Abraham passed the test with flying colors. God instructed the patriarch to sacrifice his only son, Isaac, as a burnt offering on an altar on Mount Moriah. At this juncture, Isaac was an adult.

> Isaac spoke up and said to his father Abraham, "Father?"
> "Yes, my son?" Abraham replied.
> "The fire and wood are here," Isaac said, "but where is the lamb for the burnt offering?"
> Abraham answered, "God himself will provide the lamb for the burnt offering, my son." (Genesis 22:7–8)

Abraham bound his son to the altar, and as he was ready to kill him with a knife, the angel of the Lord intervened.

> But the Angel of the Lord called out to him from heaven,
> "Abraham! Abraham!"
> "Here I am," he replied.
> "Do not lay a hand on the boy," he said, "Do not do anything to him. Now I know you have not withheld from me your son, your only son." (Genesis 22:11–12)

Abraham saw a ram in the thicket and offered the ram as a sacrifice. Abraham called the place Jehovah-jireh, meaning "the Lord will provide."

The angel of the Lord said he would bless the patriarch with many spiritual descendants. Isaac was a type of Christ in the Old Testament, while the antitype in the New Testament is Christ. God gave His only Son to die on the cross for the sins of the world. God will be Jehovah-jireh——"the Lord will provide"——for His Christians in the time of spiritual and physical need. Our response should be to love, worship, serve, and obey the Lord.

During my trip to the Holy Land in 2011, I saw several mountains, but the greatest mountain was Mount Calvary, where Jesus Christ, the Lamb of God, sacrificed His life for the redemption of the world.

Have you been exposed to COVID-19? Jehovah-jireh! Did you quit a job and are beginning a new job? Jehovah-jireh! Are you concerned about your children with COVID-19? Jehovah-jireh!

The Pillar of Fire

Exodus 14:19–21 describes God's protective hand in assisting the Israelites. Remember that they were a nomadic tribe that wandered in the wilderness for forty years until they reached the promised land. During this time, there were problems, struggles, and frustration. As our account opens, Pharaoh is pursuing the Israelites. He is going to have a rude surprise that will be disastrous to his entire army.

Israel is translated as "he struggles with God." *Peniel* means "face of God." From that day forward, Jews no longer ate the tendon attached to the socket of the hip.

The man in the above scripture is the angel of the Lord.

> He struggled with the angel and overcame him; he
> wept and begged for his favor. (Hosea 12:4)

We will never have such an experience as Jacob, who wrestled with the angel of the Lord, but we, too, have our everyday struggles and vicissitudes. As praying Christians, we should be more constant and have fervor in all of our prayer lives when we spiritualty struggle with God for an answer. The answer may not be the answer that we desire, but we must submit to the will of God in our lives. We have a Christian plaque in our home that reads, "Life is fragile. Handle with prayer."

Nota bene: Jacob's name was changed to Israel, meaning "struggled with God." We all have our struggles in one form or another. I took a course at the University of Illinois while completing my master's degree in social work, and I chose to make a study of tough love. I was amazed by the struggles and problems the parents had with their teenagers. Tough love means *tough love*; it could mean allowing a teenager to spend a night in jail to teach him a lesson. We may never have a face-to-face encounter with God, as Jacob did, but we see our wonderful Lord through the holy inspired scriptures.

"We Are Climbing Jacob's Ladder"

This hymn's origin is traced to the slave population of the United States in 1824. It portrays the struggle to reach a better place in their lives.

In Genesis 27, Jacob tricked his brother Esau twice. He was on the run and was fleeing to his uncle Laban. When he fell asleep, he had a vision where he saw angels ascending and descending from heaven, and the angel of the Lord spoke to him. The angel of the Lord was the preincarnate. Christ is the connection between heaven and earth.

God made Jacob four promises:

1. That He would be with Jacob wherever he goes.

> Then the angel of God, who had been traveling in front of Israel's army, withdrew and went behind them. The pillar of cloud also moved from in front and stood behind them, coming between the armies of Egypt and Israel. Throughout the night the cloud brought darkness to the one side and light to the other side; so neither went near the other all night. (Exodus 14:19–21)

> Neither the pillar of cloud by day nor the pillar of fire by night left its place in front of the people. (Exodus 13:22)

113

These two items were their North Star that guided God's people for forty years in the desert.

The desert is a hot spot; I lived in Tucson, Arizona, for twenty-four years, and it gets very hot, sometimes to 110 degrees. God protected the Israelites so that they could survive the scorching heat. When the cloud stopped above them, the Israelites stopped and pitched a tent. When the cloud moved, they followed. The pillar of fire kept them warm during the chill of the night desert. Through the pillars of cloud and fire, God's people witnessed the divine guidance and protection from a benevolent Lord. The pillars are a snapshot of God's faithfulness and a lesson to us that God never leaves or forsakes His believers.

Today, we do not have a cloud by day or a pillar of fire by night to guide us, but we do have the direction of God's Word that leads us in the proper direction.

Shechinah

Shechinah is derived from the Hebrew *shakhan*, "dwelling" or "setting." Some scholars have presented the idea that Shechinah is from the Greek word *parousia*, signifying "presence" or "arrival." It means divine presence.

I started my ministry in the Lutheran Church in 1958, serving two congregations, St. John's in Tyndall, South Dakota, and Our Savior's Chapel plus Gamma Delta campus work at Southern State Teachers College. During my tenure I exchanged pulpits with the pastor at Dimock, South Dakota. Preaching there was quite an experience, for there was a tall, winding stairway to the pulpit, and above the pulpit was a symbol of a cloud, exemplifying the Shechinah, or presence of God. I preached in numerous congregations, but this pulpit was extraordinary.

As Christians, we are assured of the presence of God in our lives.

> The Lord replied, My presence will go with you, and
> I will give you rest. (Exodus 33:14)

> For where two or three come together in my name,
> there am I with them. (Matthew 18:20)

Moses and the Burning Bush

Moses had been leading quite a dull life—no nightclub hopping for this eighty-year-old. At this time in his life, he probably would have been in a rest home. But God had other plans for this senior citizen. At this time, Moses was keeping watch for the sheep of his father-in-law, Jethro, at Mount Horeb in the Sinai area. Then, suddenly, out of nowhere, the angel of the Lord appeared as a voice out of a thorn bush, which was a species of acacia that was common to the Sinai area.

The angel of the Lord who spoke was the angel of the covenant—the second person of the Trinity. I imagine Moses was startled by this. I certainly would be startled by such a situation!

Moses had an investigative attitude and just had to check out this phenomenon. Twice, the angel of the Lord called out to him, "Moses, Moses," to exemplify the urgency of the situation.

> "Do not come any closer," God said. "Take off your
> sandals, for the place where you are standing is holy
> ground." Then he said, "I am the God of your father
> Abraham, the God of Isaac and the God of Jacob."
> At this, Moses hid his face, because he was afraid
> to look at God. (Exodus 3:5–6)

The angel of the Lord reiterated that he had seen the suffering of God's people in Egypt.

"So now, go, I am sending you to Pharaoh to bring
my people the Israelites out of Egypt."

But Moses said to God, "Who am I, that I
should go to Pharaoh and bring the Israelites out
of Egypt?"

And God said, "I will be with you." (Exodus
3:10–12)

Moses asked what he should tell the people.

God said to Moses, "I am who I am." This is what
you are to say to the Israelites: I AM has sent me to
you." (Exodus 3:14)

Moses tried to make excuses; he thought he was unqualified
to be God's spokesman. Even today, laypeople think that they are
unqualified to speak up and witness, but they are wrong. They are
more effective in winning souls for Christ than preachers!

The burning bush burned but was not consumed. No one can
explain it. God utilized this method in order to communicate His
wishes to Moses. God does not speak to us in a burning bush; rather,
He speaks to us through His inspired Word, which is efficacious and
has perspicuity.

Moses was instructed to remove his sandals, for he was treading
on holy ground. Previously, God was known as El, Elium, Elohim
(exalted, lofty) or Shaddaid (strong). Now it was Jehovah, "the
Existent."

Hagar

In both the Old Testament and the New Testament, the names
of the biblical people designate either their present or future activity.
Hagar, in Hebrew, means "flight."

Her account is recorded in Genesis 16:1–16. Sarai was beyond childbearing years, and Abraham was eighty-six years old. In spite of their ages, God promised them a child. Sarai ordered Abraham to have a liaison with their maidservant, Hagar. When Hagar found out that she was pregnant, she began to despise her mistress, and Sarai blamed Abraham for the situation. Sarai mistreated Hagar, and the maidservant fled into the desert. There is where the angel of the Lord found her.

> Then the angel of the Lord told her, "Go back to your mistress and submit to her." The angel added, "I will so increase your descendants that they will be too numerous to count." The angel of the Lord also said to her: "You are now with child and you will have a son. You shall name him Ishmael." (Genesis 16:9–11)

Ishmael, in Hebrew, means "God hears."

> "You are the God who sees me," for she said, "I have seen the One who sees me." (Genesis 16:13)

Interpreted from the Hebrew, it means "or seen the back of." The location was a well-called Beer Lahai Roi, from the Hebrew for "well of the Living One who sees me." Hagar's descendants are the Arab people, who are numerous and fighting over land in Palestine this very day——on my trip to the Holy Land, our docent, who was a Palestinian, mentioned this.

Jerusalem is an ancient city that is divided religiously among Christianity, Judaism, and Islam. On the day I was there, the Muslims were racing horses down the narrow cobblestones. When the minaret sounded for prayer, they stopped all activity and went to the mosque.

Hagar had her sins of pride, contempt, insubordination, and flight. Abram and Sarai were no saints; they had their sins also.

The angel of the Lord is Maleach Jehovah, meaning "one sent," or "one through whom work is executed."

Hagar was a fugitive and was in the wilderness when the angel of the Lord confronted her. We, too, wander today in the wilderness of sin. Jesus finds us and refreshes us.

In Galatians 4:21–31, Paul makes the distinction between Hagar's giving birth in the ordinary way and Isaac's being born as the result of a promise.

> Therefore, brothers, we are not children of the slave woman, but of the free woman. (Galatians 4:31)

Throughout the book of Galatians, Paul stresses that we are no longer under the Law but under grace.

> It is for freedom that Christ has set us free, Stand firm, then, and do not let yourselves be burdened again by a yoke of slavery, (Galatians 5:1)

Jacob

Jacob, in Hebrew, means "deceiver" or "supplanter." His name correctly identifies his activity to receive the birthright from his father, Isaac, by pretending to be Esau. The account of Jacob wrestling with the angel of the Lord is recorded in Genesis 32:22–32.

> So Jacob was left alone, and a man wrestled with him til daybreak. When the man saw that he could not over-power him, he touched the socket of Jacob's hip so that his hip was wrenched as he wrestled with the man. Then the man said, me go, for it is daybreak."
>
> But Jacob replied, "I will not let you go unless you bless me."

The man asked him, "What is your name?"

"Jacob," he answered.

Then the man said, "Your name will no longer be Jacob, but Isarel, because you have struggled with God and with men have overcome."

Jacob said, "Please tell me your name."

But he replied, "Why do you ask my name?" Then he blessed him there."

So Jacob called the place Peniel, saying, "It is because I saw God face to face, and yet my life was spared." (Genesis 32:24–30)

2. That He would guide and protect Jacob in his pilgrimage.
3. That He would bring Jacob back to the promised land.
4. That He would renew the covenant He made to Abraham and restated to Isaac and Jacob

> We are climbing Jacob's ladder,
> We are climbing Jacob's ladder,
> We are climbing Jacob's ladder,
> Soldiers of the cross.
> Sinner, do you love my Jesus?
> Sinner, do you love my Jesus?
> Sinner, do you love my Jesus?
> Soldiers of the cross.
> If you love Him, why not serve Him?
> If you love Him, why not serve Him?
> If you love Him, why not serve Him?
> Soldiers of the cross.[30]

What about your daily prayers? Have you pleaded with the Lord for something very special in your life? You probably have,

---

[30] Hymnary.org Worship and Service Hymnal.

and maybe it seemed that the Lord didn't answer as you wanted. Too often in our prayers, we try to bargain with God and offer plans A, B, or C to help God determine the solution to our prayer. Our Lord doesn't need our help. He answers our prayers with the possible plan Z, which would be better for us. We look at things mostly temporally, while God looks at the situation eternally. What an omniscient God we have! How is your prayer life? Did your prayer life increase as you matured as a child of God?

Gideon

The biblical account of Gideon is recorded in Judges 6:11–40. The name *Gideon*, from the Hebrew, means "tree-feller," and "the mighty warrior." Note that my last name is *Feller.* I am a Feller and German but not famous, as is Gideon, the tree-feller. The names of the Judges in the Bible denote the type of job God had planned for them. When God appointed the judges in Israel, God specified which enemy each judge was to conquer. Gideon's task was planned against the Midianites.

During my travels to Greece in 2010 and 2012, I visited Corinth. When we visited a museum, the docent informed our tour that the Greeks were smart people in many ways. They retained the beautiful white marble statue of their ruler but made the heads out of plaster and changed them when a new ruler reigned. Not so with the judges. Their task for life was to defeat the enemy that God designated.

Scriptures relate that God not only saw their previous oppression under Egypt but with the oppressor Midian as well. The angel of the Lord appeared to Gideon while he was threshing wheat in a winepress.

> When the angel of the Lord appeared to Gideon, he said, "The Lord is with you, mighty warrior."
>
> "But sir," Gideon replied, "if the Lord is with us, why has all this happened to us?"

The Lord turned to him and said, "Go in the strength you have and save Israel out of Midian's hand. Am I not sending you?"

"But Lord," Gideon asked, "how can I save Israel? My clan is the weakest in Manasseh, and I am the least in my family."

The Lord answered, "I will be with you, and you will strike down the Midianites as if they were but one man," (Judges 6:12–16)

Gideon then prepared an offering to the Lord.

With the tip of the staff that was in his hand, the angel of the Lord touched the meat and the unleavened bread. Fire flared from the rock, consuming the meat and the bread. And the angel of the Lord disappeared. (Judges 6:21)

Gideon, as a judge, was commanded by God to defeat the Midianites as well as the Amalekites. He obeyed and took charge as a mighty warrior.

When Gideon realized that it was the angel of the Lord, he exclaimed, "Sovereign Lord! I have seen the angel of the Lord face to face!" (Judges 6:22)

Gideon wanted to test the Lord. Gideon said he would put fleece on the threshing floor. In the morning, if there was dew only on the fleece and all the ground was dry, that would be God's sign that Gideon would be victorious over the Midianites. The next morning, Gideon found dew only on the fleece, and he wrung out a bowlful of water.

Putting Out the Fleece

What about you? Do you put out the fleece in your life in order to determine God's will for you? It's sad to say, but a lot of people use a Ouija board to determine their fortune. This is wrong and contrary to the Bible. We must always trust in our Lord and lean upon His direction in our lives. Are you putting out the fleece? God works through people and events in our lives.

God directed Gideon to choose soldiers for his army. Gideon determined his army by the men who lapped the water from the brook like dogs. Three hundred men were chosen. When I was in the Holy Land, our guide took us to this same brook where Gideon was directed to choose his army to defeat the Midianites.

Paul, the apostle, assures us, "No, in all things we are more than conquerors through him who loved us" (Romans 8:37).

> I can do everything through him who gives me strength. (Philippians 4:13)

From the biblical account of Gideon, we see that the angel of the Lord is the preincarnate Son of God.

Joshua

Joshua is an interesting person in the Old Testament. His name, from the Hebrew, means "the Lord is salvation" and "a soldier of the Lord."

> Now when Joshua was near Jericho, he looked up and saw a man standing in front of him with a drawn sword in his hand. Joshua went up to him and asked, "Are you for us or for our enemies?" "Neither," he replied, "but as commander of the army of the Lord I have now come." (Joshua 5:13–14)

The angel of Lord (Christ himself) was the commander of the army of God. This term registered with Joshua, for he was a soldier of the Lord, Joshua was to demonstrate his obedience and his humility by removing his sandals, for he was on holy ground when he stood before the Lord. At this point, he gives the command and directions to besiege the city of Jericho.

Joshua's army was directed to march around the city of Jericho for six days, with seven priests carrying seven trumpets, marching before the ark of the covenant. On the seventh day, they marched around blowing their trumpets. They exclaimed, "Shout! For the Lord has given you the city!" (Joshua 5:16b). Jericho was decimated.

I visited Jericho on my trip to the Holy Land. Jericho is famous for the sycamore tree where little Zacchaeus climbed to see Jesus.

> When Jesus reached the spot, he looked up and said
> to him Zacchaeus, come down immediately. I must
> stay at your house today. (Luke 19:5)

Joshua is a type of Christ. Joshua, commander of the Israelites, is commander as the type, while Christ is the anti-type in the New Testament as the commander in chief of the Christian army of God. As Joshua led the children of Israel to the promised land of Canaan, flowing with milk and honey, so Jesus leads us to heaven through faith in His most precious blood.

"Onward, Christian Soldiers"

This hymn was written by Sabine Baring-Gould in 1865, the year of President Lincoln's Emancipation Proclamation. The words are based on Paul's words to Timothy: "Endure hardship with us like a good soldier of Christ Jesus" (2 Timothy 2:3). The music was added by Arthur Sullivan in 1871 to the tune of "St. Gertrude." Later, the Salvation Army used this favorite hymn as a processional.

This hymn was written as a processional hymn for children in the parish of Horbury Bridge in Yorkshire, England. Gould's first intention was to use the title of "Hymn for Procession with Cross and Banners."

In 1941, when Winston Churchill and Franklin D. Roosevelt met on the HMS *Prince of Wales*, Prime Minister Churchill chose the hymn for one of his radio broadcasts.

"Onward, Christian Soldiers" was sung at the funeral of President Dwight D. Eisenhower in 1969. It has been sung in numerous Christian churches throughout the ages.

Bokim

> The angel of the Lord went up from Gilgal to Bokim[31] and said, "I brought you up out of Egypt and led you into the land that I swore to give to your forefathers, I said "I will never break my covenant with you, and you shall not make a covenant with the people in this land, but you will break down their altars" Yet you have disobeyed me. Why have you done this? Now therefore I tell you that I will not drive them out before you; they will be thorns in your sides and their gods will be a snare to you." When the angel of the Lord had spoken these things to all of the Israelites, the people wept aloud, and they called that place Bokim. There they offered sacrifices to the Lord." (Judges 2:1–5)

Here, after the angel of the Lord reprimanded them, they wept tears of contrition. Sin should drive us, even today, to contrition to confess our sins before God in true repentance. The Israelites were faithful for a while and later were recalcitrant, falling back to their old ways. The heathen gods were beckoning to them with all sorts of temptations. Today, as Christians, we face the challenge of the

---

[31] Bokim, signifies weepers.

temptation to slip away from God by our sins. God, in His mercy, calls us back by His love.

Isaiah Predicts Vengeance and Redemption

Isaiah, the prophet, states,

> "I have trodden down the winepress alone; from the nations no one was with me trampeled them in my anger and trod them down in my wrath; their blood spattered my garments, and I stained all my clothing. For the day of vengeance was in my heart, and the year of my redemption has come." (Isaiah 63:3–4)

Isaiah is referring to the judgment of God upon Idumaea. God will be the mighty warrior who will fight for God's people.

> He said, "Surely they are my people, sons who will not be false to me"; so he became their Savior. In all their distress he too was distressed, and the angel of the presence saved them." (Isaiah 63:8–9)

The "angel of the presence" refers to the angel of the Lord (the preincarnate Logns). Today, our God will go to battle for His church and Christians. Christians must be equipped with special armor, as described in Ephesians 6:10–17. Paul states that we must put on the whole armor of God and not just part of it. Ancient soldiers would dress correctly with the full panoply of God before a battle. Arm yourself, Christians!

Abraham Welcomes Three Visitors

Genesis 18:1–15 records that three visitors appeared to Abraham at the umbrageous oak of Mamre. At first, Abraham surmised that they were just strangers, but one was the incarnate Christ and the other two mere angels. Abraham certainly had the spiritual gift of hospitality, for he personally prepared a sumptuous meal for the three visitors. Abraham had three hundred servants who could have prepared the meal, but Abraham took charge personally of the meal preparation. We can learn from this story to practice cheerfulness and promptitude as Christians.

The angel of the Lord (Christ) announced that Sarah would give birth to a son in her old age. When Sarah heard this news, she laughed. Immediately, the angel of the Lord interrogated Abraham about Sarah's laughter. Jehovah gave the great news that Sarah (age ninety) and Abraham (age one hundred) would be parents of a son. Jehovah always keeps His promises, for He is the covenant Lord.

But what about humankind? Do we keep all of our promises that we make to other people? We are promise-breakers. I cite promises we make to our children but never plan to keep them. A man and a woman promise at the altar of God "til death do we part." No! Divorce is on the rise. The ratio is one out three marriages is dissolved by divorce.

Jehovah stated to Sarah, "Is anything too hard for the Lord?" (Genesis 18:14). As humans, we are limited in things that we can do. We can drive cars, calculate our finances, and do some difficult jobs. But our God can do everything. We are reminded of the words,

> The Lord your God is a merciful God; He will not forsake you, neither destroy you, nor forget the covenant of your fathers which He sware to them. (Deuteronomy 4:31)

We see the theophany of God at Mamre. It was a divine visit to Abraham that demonstrated a remarkable proof of the divine condescension. Also, it exemplified a striking adumbration of the incarnation of Christ, as well as the gracious visits of God to His people. In this account, we also learn that the other two angels assumed human visage. Jehovah was preparing the angels to destroy Sodom and Gomorrah in the very near future.

David

In 1 Chronicles 21:1–20 we read the account of King David, who ordered Joab to take a census of the fighting men in Israel. Joab made the count and reported back to David. The report stated that there were 1,100,000 fighting men who could handle a sword. God was unhappy with David's order to count the number of fighting men, and God punished Israel.

> Then David said to God, "I have sinned greatly by doing this. Now, I beg you take away the guilt of your servant. I have done a foolish thing." (1 Chronicles 21:8)

The Lord gave David three options: (1) three years of famine, (2) three months of being swept away before his enemies, with their swords overtaking him, (3) pestilence throughout the land. God was unhappy with David's command due to David's regal pride that he was a great warrior with a mighty army. There were consequences of sin, even with David's contrition. God sent a pestilence that killed over five million people.

> "David looked up and saw the angel of the Lord standing between heaven and earth, with a drawn sword in his hand extended over Jerusalem. Then David and the elders clothed in sackcloth, fell facedown." (1 Chronicles 21:16)

David was commanded to build an altar and make a sacrifice at the threshing floor of Araunah the Jebusite. The Lord put His sword back into His sheath. Repentance is important in our lives as Christians. Daily, we should confess our sins and ask God for forgiveness. God forgives our sins through faith in Christ as our personal Savior. Repentance, in Greek, is *metanoia,* or change of mind. This means a 180-degree turn—turning from sin and turning to God. This is repentance. The Greek verb *metanoeo* appears in Luke nine times; in Acts, five times; and twelve times in Revelation.

Manoah

This is another account where the angel of the Lord appears in scriptures. Manoah's wife was barren, and according to the Jews, being childless was unacceptable and had a stigma attached to it. The angel of the Lord promised that Manoah's wife would have a son and name him Samson, which means "sun-man" or "the weak strong man" in Hebrew. Several times in the Old Testament, the term *man* is ascribed to the angel of the Lord until the recipients realize who he is. Manoah's wife inquired, "Who is this man of God?"

> Then the woman went to her husband and told him, "a man of God came to me. He looked like an angel of God, very awesome, I didn't ask him where he came from, and he didn't tell me his name." (Judges 13:6)

The angel of the Lord announced that Samson would be a Nazirite. Samuel was also a Nazirite. The requirements for a Nazirite are recorded in Numbers 6:1–21. The Law required the following to be a Nazirite:

1. Abstain from all wine and anything else made from the grape vine plant.
2. Refrain from cutting hair on one's head but allow the head's hair to grow.
3. Not become ritually impure by contact with corpses or graves, even those of family members.

The Nazirite would give three offerings to God:

1. He would immerse himself in a mikvah (ritual bath) and offer a lamb as a burnt offering. It was *olah.*
2. He would give a ewe as a sin offering (*hatat*)
3. He would give a ram as a peace offering (*shelamim*).

A basket of unleavened bread, grain offerings, and drink offerings followed. They would shave their heads in the outer courtyard of the temple and place the hair on the fire as the peace offering. The Hebrew word for Nazirite is *nazir,* meaning "consecrated" or "separated." There were two types of Nazirites: (1) one who made a vow for thirty days and (2) a permanent Nazirite for his entire life. John the Baptist in the New Testament was a Nazirite.

Both Manoah and his wife kept asking their visitor his name. The angel of Lord stated that his name was beyond understanding. Scholars interpret this term as "wonderful." Isaiah 9:6 mentions Christ as the wonderful counselor. After Manoah offered up a goat, the angel of the Lord ascended in the flame. What were the reactions of Manoah and his wife? Manoah realized the visitor was the angel of the Lord and said they were doomed to die. His wife countered and said that if the Lord meant to kill them, He would not have accepted their offerings.

The angel of the Lord (the preincarnate Logos) appeared to God's people in the time of need. Just think of this couple's many prayers that ascended to heaven to have a famous son.

CHAPTER ELEVEN

CLOSING PRAYER

The Praying Hands

There is a false story about the history of the praying hands. The false history states that Albrecht Durer came from a large family of eighteen siblings. Both he and his brother wanted to be artists. With no money for art school, the brother worked in the mines, where he developed gnarled hands. Albrecht sketched his brother, and that sketch today and for the past five hundred years has been in museums, on plaques, and on the tombstone of Andy Warhol.

What is the true history of the praying hands? In 1507, Albrecht Durer was commissioned by Jacob Heller to paint a triptych altar piece on the assumption and coronation of the Virgin Mary for a Catholic Church in Frankfurt, Germany.

This project was not completed until 1509. Durer had disagreements with his patron due a delay of reimbursement.

A Prayer

My Father for another night of quiet sleep and rest.
And for the joys of morning light
Your own dear name be blessed.
O help me Lord this day to be your own dear child
And follow You.
And lead me Savior by your hand
Until I reach the heavenly land.
Amen.
Soli Deo Gloria

ANSWERS TO THE ANGEL QUOTIENT QUIZ

1. T
2. T
3. F
4. T
5. F
6. T
7. T
8. F
9. T
10. F
11. F
12. F

Old Testament Examples

1. Adam and Eve's expulsion (Genesis 3:24)
2. Daniel in lion's den (Daniel 6:18–29)
3. Sodom and Gomorrah (Genesis 19:1–13)
4. Shadrach. Meshach. Abednego (Daniel 3:24–28)
5. 185,000 Assyrians (2 Kings 19:35–36)
6. Elisha (1 Kings 6:13–17)
7. Elijah (1 Kings 19:1–9)
8. Balaam (Numbers 22:21–35)

New Testament Examples

1. Zechariah (Luke 1:13)
2. Mary (Luke 1:35)
3. Shepherds (Luke 2:11)
4. Temptation (Matthew 4:1–11)
5. Gethsemane (Luke 22:43)

BIBLIOGRAPHY

Angeology: The Doctrine of Angels, Bible.org

Appleboon, Cogan, Klastersky, Mount Sinai School of Medicine, 2007, Los Angeles. Job of the Bible: Leprosy or Scabies?

Brecht, Martin, Martin Luther. tr James L. Schaaf Phaldelphia: Fortress Press, 1985–93, 1:466.

Graham, Billy, Angels: God's Secret Agents, Doubleday & Company, Inc., Garden City, New York, 1975

Halley, Henry Hampton, Halley's Bible Handbook, Zondervan Publishing House, Grand Rapids, Michigan, 2000.

Henley, William, Ernest, Book of Verses, Life & Death (echoes) 1888, England)

Hoenecke, Adelf, Evangelical Lutheran Dogmatics, Northwestern Publishing House, Milwaukee, Wisconsin, 1999

Hymnary.org

Kold, Robert, Wenget, Book of Concord; The Confessions of the Evangelical Lutheran Church, Minneapolis; Augsburg, Fortress, 200,486

Koehler, Edward W.A., A Summary of Christian Doctrine, Koehler Publishing Company, River Forest, ILL. 1939

Luther, Martin, Luther's Small Catechism, Concordia Publishing House, St Louis. Mo. 1986

Mounce, William D & Robert H., Greek and Engliah Interlinar Zondervan, Grand Rapids, Michigan, 2011

Nestle, D. Erwin, Novum Testamentum Greece, Stuttgart, Germany, Privileqierte Wurttembergische Biblanstalt, 1950

Newport, Why Are Americans Losing Confidence in Organized Religion?

Pew Research Center, Washington D.C.

Pieper, Francis, Christian Dogmatics, Concordia Publishing House, SL Louis. Mo. Vol. 1950, Vol. III 1953

Ryden, E.E., The Story of Christian Hymnody, Augustana Press, Rock Island, Illinois, 1959

Strong, James, The New Strong's Complete Dictionary of Bible Words, Thomas Nelson Publishers, Nashville, TN. 1996

Strong, James, The New Strong's Exhaustive Concordance of the Bible, Thomas Nelson, Nashville, TN., 1995.

Unger Merrill F., Unger's Bible Handbook, Moody Press,

Vine, W.E., Vine's Expository Dictionary of Old and New Testament Words, Thomas Nelson, Nashville, TN. 1997

Wikipedia

Worldwise Hymns, 2010/04/20, Erastus-Johnson Born

Printed in the United States
by Baker & Taylor Publisher Services

Printed in the United States
by Baker & Taylor Publisher Services